# The Sm
## & Morrissey

CH00731537

BY JOHNNY ROGAN

Copyright © 1995 Johnny Rogan
Published by Omnibus Press (A Division of Book Sales Limited)

Edited by Chris Charlesworth
Cover & Book designed by 4i Limited
Picture research by Johnny Rogan & Nikki Russell

**ISBN: 0.7119.4900.X Order No: OP 47768**

*Exclusive Distributors*
Book Sales Limited, 8/9 Frith Street, London W1V 5TZ, UK.
Music Sales Corporation, 257 Park Avenue South, New York, NY 10010, USA.
Music Sales Pty Limited, 120 Rothschild Avenue, Rosebery, NSW 2018, Australia.

*To the Music Trade only:*
Music Sales Limited, 8/9 Frith Street, London W1V 5TZ, UK.

*Photo credits:* all photographs courtesy of LFI & Barry Plummer.

Every effort has been made to trace the copyright holders of the photographs in this book but one or two were unreachable. We would be grateful if the photographers concerned would contact us.

Printed in the United Kingdom by Ebenezer Baylis & Son, Worcester.

A catalogue record for this book is available from the British Library.

# contents

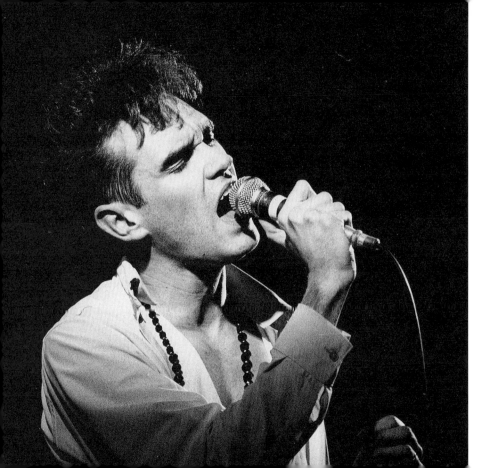

# introduction and acknowledgements

This book is intended as a listening guide to the CD album releases of The Smiths, plus Morrissey and Johnny Marr's post-1987 work. Over the years, The Smiths' importance has been established and most critics now respect them as one of the most intriguing groups of the Eighties. Theirs is a formidable body of work forged over an intense five year period.

As well as the standard album releases, the group recorded a wealth of singles, B-sides and radio sessions, a large proportion of which were captured on various compilations. Putting together this guide has given me the opportunity to sit down and listen to the entire canon once more, as well as considering the comments of various members on particular songs. Where possible, I have sneaked in a few new facts, snippets, fresh interviews and perspectives to add to the reader's appreciation.

It is salutary to consider that Morrissey has now been a soloist longer than the entire lifetime of The Smiths. Soon, the number of songs he has written will eclipse the total credited to Morrissey/Marr. The same could not be said of his erstwhile partner. Marr has been involved in a variety of projects since leaving the group, but the results have been less prolific than we might have expected back in 1987.

Similarly, Mike Joyce and Andy Rourke have taken much time in finding a suitable vehicle for their respective recording plans, although they too have guested with a range of artistes since the demise of The Smiths. Craig Gannon appeared to retire from touring and recording for awhile, but has since teamed up with his former colleague Terry Hall. The Smiths' legacy goes on.

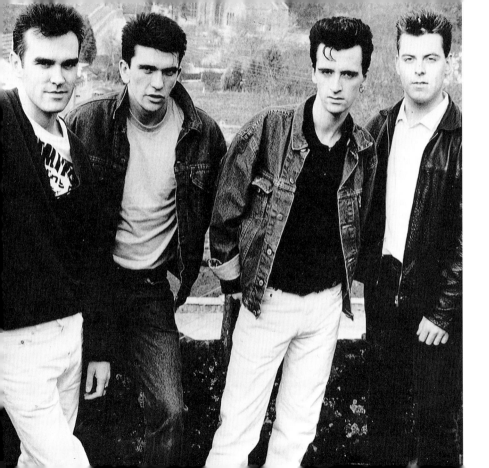

In compiling and writing this book, I owe much to the input of interviewees Johnny Marr, Andy Rourke, Mike Joyce, Craig Gannon, Vini Reilly, Matt Johnson and original bassist Dale, plus producers John Porter and Stephen Street. There are scores of other people I have spoken to over the past seven years whose memories and insights are greatly appreciated. For a full roll call readers should consult the acknowledgements sections of *Morrissey & Marr: The Severed Alliance* and *The Smiths: A Visual Documentary*.

JOHNNY ROGAN

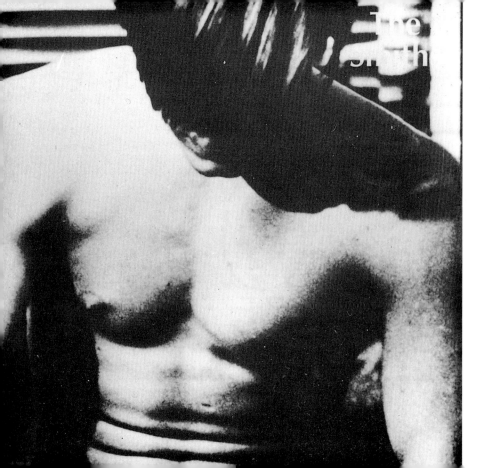

# smiths albums
## THE SMITHS

ORIGINAL ISSUE: ROUGH TRADE RECORDS, ROUGH 61, FEBRUARY 1984. REISSUED ROUGH CD 61, OCTOBER 1986.

CURRENT ISSUE: WEA 4509 91892-2, NOVEMBER 1993, FEBRUARY 1995.

The Smiths' début album was recorded on a £20,000 budget, amid indecision and several last minute changes of heart. Although the group had been playing frequently throughout the year, their studio experience was minimal and this was reflected in the quality of the initial recordings. Original producer Troy Tate was devastated to learn that his contributions were not deemed worthy of release and the entire project was to be handed over to John Porter.

The problems did not end there. Morrissey's reluctance to re-record or over-dub certain tracks meant that the album retained a minimalist feel, which was not always to The Smiths' advantage. With time and money at a premium, work was rapidly completed and expectation was high when the album reached the public in February 1984.

Many critics were expecting an instant classic to rank alongside the acclaimed début albums of years past, such as 'The Doors' and 'Roxy Music'. Alas, the album's impact was severely qualified by the bargain basement sound and understandably muted production. Morrissey attempted to "talk up" the album in interviews, extravagantly referring to it as a landmark in the history of pop music. Behind the hyperbole, though, he realised that The Smiths had not done themselves full justice.

Critical reservations aside, there was no denying that The Smiths' début highlighted the arrival of a formidable songwriting partnership. It was clear that they were a group well versed in rock tradition but armed with a keen knowledge of the power of simple pop music. Morrissey's engagingly ambiguous lyrics subverted the entire package with lashings of camp knowing and subtle irony. His vocal, still very flat and occasionally uncertain, could nevertheless shift from a deadpan moan to a hyena howl or excruciating falsetto at a moment's notice.

Equally importantly, they looked the part. Marr could still play the teenage prodigy with a strong sense of rock fashion. Morrissey , by contrast, used spectacles and flowers as anti-rock star accoutrements to bolster his image as the bedsit misanthrope blessed with unlikely fame. The public perception of Rourke and Joyce as solid, dependable, unselfish players testified to a sense of camaraderie that made The Smiths special. Even their artwork was carefully conceived to reflect Morrissey's affinity with gay culture as well as serving as an ongoing gallery of his favourite icons. With all that added to the press controversy which infrequently dogged Morrissey, it was clear that The Smiths could look forward to a long and eventful career.

## REEL AROUND THE FOUNTAIN

It is difficult to dissociate The Smiths' opening album track from the paedophile debate pre-dating its release. *The Sun*'s sensationalist reporting of its theme brought a strident defence from Morrissey who insisted that the composition contained no hidden innuendo. Despite his stated intention, there is a still a strong underlying erotic frisson in this tale of innocence under threat. In keeping with the ambiguous theme, it is interesting to note that Marr originally composed the song as a cross between the dark introspection of Joy Division and the upbeat optimism of Jimmy Jones' 'Handy Man'. Although The Smiths were reluctant to employ session musicians on their records, producer John Porter managed to persuade them to use pianist Paul Carrack "to add a bit of colour" to the track.

## YOU'VE GOT EVERYTHING NOW

A classic example of Morrissey's acerbic wit, this song satirised his materialist-minded contemporaries. In interviews he spoke frequently of the horrors of working for a living, but his amusing quotes pale alongside the instant aphorisms featured in many of the songs on this album. Here, conflicting feelings of jealousy, aloofness, arrogance and self-abasement mingle to startling effect, reinforced by the straightforward, uncomplicated arrangement.

## MISERABLE LIE

This was often used as the closing song in The Smiths' early live sets and it is not too difficult to hear why. Morrissey sounds like a demented punk imitating Tiny Tim as he stretches his vocal cords to reach an unholy falsetto. The theme of lost romantic idealism fitted in well with the remaining tracks, posing the inevitable question about the autobiographical content of the songs.

## PRETTY GIRLS MAKE GRAVES

Morrissey's love of gender play provides a tragi-comic feel to many of these songs. Here, he subverts traditional male/female roles to present the female as sexually voracious and her male prey as a helpless innocent. Although there is a hint of misogyny in the treatment, the predominant tone is playful, with continually self-deprecating references thrown in at every opportunity.

## THE HAND THAT ROCKS THE CRADLE

One of the first songs written by Morrissey/Marr, this was played at their initial rehearsal with guitarist Steve Pomfret who, shortly before, had introduced the pair to each other. Marr's compelling arrangement may sound familiar for it was borrowed from Patti Smith's 'Kimberly'. The intriguing lyrics are arguably Morrissey's most unusual to date. His approach is almost cinematic as he focuses on innocuous objects which are magically transformed into disturbing images. Entering the child's imagination, he adds an air of inexplicable mystery as we successively witness a piano playing in an empty room, wardrobes disguised as birds and the sudden horror movie image of a bloodied cleaver. The sense of danger is hardly alleviated by the narrator whose obsessive, determinedly self-sacrificial love seems disturbingly suffocating. The Al Jolson inspired coda "climb upon my knee sonny boy" serves as both a poignant expression of innocence and additional fuel to those who detect paedophiliac connotations in the composition.

## THIS CHARMING MAN

If you happen to own the Warner Brothers re-issue of this album, then this bonus hit single is included. On all previous British CD and album releases it was not issued, although it appeared on American pressings. For some, it will seem a little strange to hear the original album with an extra song stuck in the middle, but there is no denying the power of this, the group's first major hit single. When it was re-issued by WEA in 1992, the song climbed to number 8, the highest position ever achieved by a Smiths' single. For a fuller discussion consult 'Hatful Of Hollow'.

## STILL ILL

One of the longest running songs in The Smiths' live set, this was Morrissey's paean to hypochondria and self reliance. As Marr wittily noted: "You listen to a song like 'Still Ill' and the title alone sums up Morrissey". The championing of the outsider was a key feature of the singer's appeal and opened up a wide market for The Smiths. The allusive lyrics, with their cod philosophical speculations ("Does the body rule the mind or does the mind rule the body?") merely enhanced the mystery of Morrissey.

## HAND IN GLOVE

Originally cut at Strawberry Studios for a couple of hundred pounds and remixed by John Porter, this served as The Smiths' first single. Marr opens the recording with a harmonica break, just as The Beatles had done with their début 'Love Me Do'. Morrissey's strained vocal eulogises a love threatened by public disapproval and mockery. The words proved equally appealing to star-crossed lovers, budding adolescent romantics and yet to be declared homosexuals. Underpinning the lyric was Morrissey's perennial self-effacing irony, for in the final couplet of the song his great love is exposed as little more than an ephemeral fantasy.

## WHAT DIFFERENCE DOES IT MAKE?

Improbably based on Jo Jo Gunne's 'Run Run Run', this R&B-influenced foray took The Smiths to number 12 in the UK charts. Despite its commercial success, Morrissey was never happy with the recording which was primarily championed by Marr. "We explored overdubbing guitars and there's probably about 14 or 15 on there," noted producer John Porter. Although the song featured in the group's live performances at the time, it was soon dropped, and Morrissey has never said a good word about it since.

## I DON'T OWE YOU ANYTHING

Mike Joyce describes this as "a massively powerful track and one of the most powerful that Morrissey has ever done". It may be neither, but it always worked well in concert and was deemed suitable for one of the group's several radio sessions of the period.

## SUFFER LITTLE CHILDREN

This moving and unjustly controversial tribute to the victims of the Moors Murderers was one of the first lyrics that Marr saw when he visited Morrissey's house. He was so impressed by the composition that he rapidly composed the lustrous melody which gave the lyrics even greater poignancy. An early line-up of The Smiths recorded the song as a demo when it was still titled 'Over The Moors'. Original bassist Dale played me the prototype version which features a more striking double track vocal. Marr also recorded some playground noises which were not deemed suitable for the album but would have added marvellously to the overall effect. It would appear that The Smiths only played this song once live which suggests that Morrissey may have regarded it as too personal for regular public exposure.

# The Smiths

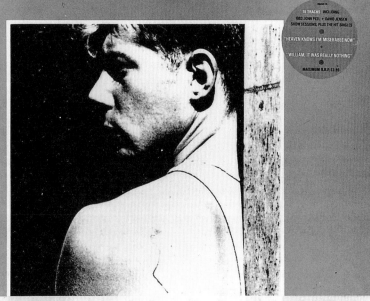

**" H A T F U L   O F   H O L L O W "**

# HATFUL OF HOLLOW

ORIGINAL ISSUE: ROUGH TRADE RECORDS, ROUGH 76, NOVEMBER 1984. REISSUED: ROUGH CD 76, DECEMBER 1985.

CURRENT ISSUE: WEA 4509-91893, NOVEMBER 1993, FEBRUARY 1995.

The release of 'Hatful Of Hollow' was partly a result of fan pressure and a reaction against some of the shortcomings of the first album. During their first year of fame, The Smiths had appeared on several BBC radio sessions and home-made tapes of these were now exchanging hands among their more avid supporters. Morrissey was impressed by the number of letters he received begging for their official release and saw the project as a perfect opportunity to atone for the shortcomings of the début album. Selections from the BBC sessions, complemented by several rare flip sides, provided an opportunity to hear The Smiths in their primitive glory.

The release was, in some respects, an audacious move. At such a crucial early stage in their career, few groups would have sanctioned what amounted to an archival recording. Most releases of this nature tended to be posthumous. Even Beatles' fans had to wait 24 years after the group's break-up before the BBC radio sessions were deemed fit for the marketplace. If The Smiths had been signed to a major label it is probable that 'Hatful Of Hollow' would never have been sanctioned. The beauty of Rough Trade was that it had a willingness to take risks and a firm understanding of the marketplace at which it was aiming.

The decision to issue the album at mid-price complete with a striking gatefold sleeve was inspired. At nearly an hour in length and with 16 songs to savour, the package was an irresistible bargain for those still curious about The Smiths but not yet willing to risk paying out for a full price album. Far from damaging The Smiths' career trajectory, this unexpected compilation kept them in the public eye and its ascent into the Top 5 emphasised the sagacity of its release. Those lucky enough to hear the group for the first time could hardly have had a better or more economical introduction.

## WILLIAM, IT WAS REALLY NOTHING

This slight, urban comic drama is one of Morrissey's most delicately understated songs. The scenario is almost certainly borrowed from Keith Waterhouse's *Billy Liar*, in which William Fisher fights a losing battle to escape from the shackles of provincial life by dreaming of a script-writing career in London. For Morrissey, the theme had an acutely autobiographical significance. Only a few years before, he was walking the streets of Manchester, dreaming of a pop star fame which seemed as illusory as Billy Liar's fantasies. Marr's accompanying arrangement served as a text book lesson in effective simplicity. "'William' is quite a whimsical song," he noted. "I don't think it's broken all the rules in pop music, but to start with a short verse and then follow it with three choruses is quite good..."

## WHAT DIFFERENCE DOES IT MAKE?

This less measured version of the song met with Morrissey's preference. The most noticeable difference is the more prominent drum work which, not surprisingly, appealed to Mike Joyce. As he notes: "The Peel session was myself and Andy playing the way I wanted to and at the time that sounded very indie, very busy, attacking and aggressive. The one that came out on the first album was a bit more solid. It pinned down the beat a lot easier for people to understand on the dance floor... The Peel version was the way I wanted it to be and the John Porter version is the way he wanted it to be. John Porter thought he was right that it should be a more solid laid down track as opposed to a jumbled up sound of rhythm."

## THESE THINGS TAKE TIME

Neuroses, insecurity and a sprinkling of gallows humour characterised Morrissey's latest ode to unrealisable love. As ever, bathos is used to humorous effect as we are taken from the holy vision of a sacred wunderkind to the sordid site of a disused railway line within the space of two lines.

## THIS CHARMING MAN

When Rough Trade founder Geoff Travis heard this radio session, he immediately suggested that this song be put forward as the next Smiths' single in place of the controversial

'The Hand That Rocks The Cradle'. It is not too difficult to understand why. With its infectious melody and tart lyrics this was undoubtedly the group's most commercial offering to date. The reference to a "jumped up pantry boy" was allegedly borrowed from the film *Sleuth* but what struck most listeners was Marr's chiming guitar work. Morrissey's deliberately elliptical verses featured strong homo-erotic undertones for those with a knowing eye.

## HOW SOON IS NOW?

Sire Records' supremo Seymour Stein called this "the 'Stairway To Heaven' of the Eighties". Unquestionably one of The Smiths' most loved and enduring songs, its recording history was a veritable comedy of errors. John Porter produced this version on 1 August for broadcast on the *John Peel Show* eight days later. The atmosphere in the studio was highly charged with the group bathed in red light in order to enhance the eerie mood. Marr plays a brooding arrangement which he described as "a perfect cross between a sweaty, swamp backing track and an intense wired shock every few bars". Morrissey's opening lines are among his best and the lyrics transform feelings of self-pity into a triumphant cry of defiance in favour of the shy, awkward, maladjusted and unloved.

John Porter immediately recognised the song's hit potential but was mortified to discover that the track was not even deemed suitable for official release on a B-side. Instead, an alternate version of the song was tucked away as an extra track on the 12-inch version of 'William, It Was Really Nothing'. "They just threw it away," Porter lamented. Three months after the release of 'Hatful Of Hollow', 'How Soon Is Now?' was belatedly issued as an A-side in the UK but, by then, its impact was severely lessened and it peaked at a lowly number 25. Geoff Travis still hoped that the song might break The Smiths in the USA, but despite considerable airplay on college radio, it failed to dent the charts.

Marr's backing track remained a favourite of radio broadcasters in search of a theme and the song's lasting appeal was indicated by its reappearance as a sample on Soho's 1991 hit, 'Hippiechick'. Morrissey and Marr responded to the authorised sampling by successfully securing 25 per cent of the royalties from Soho's recording.

## HANDSOME DEVIL

First recorded live as the B-side to 'Hand In Glove', this version was taped at the BBC on 18 May 1983. Its playful gender switching caused furrowed brows to ponder over its homo-erotic content, while the inclusion of the phrase "mammary glands" prompted a counter offensive heterosexual reading. For the tabloids and Lolita hunters it provided a strong case for a paedophiliac interpretation, made more plausible by the arch references to helping a boy get through his exams, possibly with the assistance of oral sex. Even the S&M brigade could find some excitement with the references to cracking whips. Here, the celibate singer provided his listeners with a cornucopia of catch-all sexuality. Interestingly, Morrissey's response to the speculation was disingenuous in the extreme. Completely ignoring the explicit sexuality throughout the composition, he directed listeners to the final two lines which he naively termed "the essence of the song". Not for the first time, his simplistic view remained largely unchallenged.

## HAND IN GLOVE

The one track on the album exclusively pro-

duced by The Smiths, this was a chance to revisit memories of the group's origins and first attempts at recording. The sound is muddied and the group choose a fade rather than the dramatic close later featured on the first album. Throughout The Smiths' career Morrissey always lavished praise on this song and its chart failure encouraged him to persuade Sandie Shaw to right the wrongs of pop history by belatedly taking a cover version into the Top 30.

## STILL ILL

Positively primitive compared to the version that graced their first album, this radio session revealed Marr in uncertain mood and suggested that the song was still at the rehearsal stage. This was also one of the few occasions when Marr provided a harmonica introduction. Not surprisingly, the instrument was replaced when they entered the recording studio.

## HEAVEN KNOWS
## I'M MISERABLE NOW

This was the song that, more than any, equated Morrissey with the word "miserable". Yet, it was far from his bleakest work and amid the litany of discontent there is at least an acceptance of temporary happiness – albeit when drunk. Morrissey's vocal is impressively confident while Marr sounds as though he has been locked in a room and forcibly fed a glut of Sixties' instrumental albums.

## THIS NIGHT HAS OPENED MY EYES

This is the one song on the compilation previously unavailable in any form. The composition was inspired by Shelagh Delaney's *A Taste Of Honey* and the lines "I dreamt about you last night and I fell out of bed twice" were taken direct from the play. The recording was done in the wake of the paedophile controversy, so producer Roger Pusey was wary of broadcasting anything too offensive. "He was told to vet the lyrics," claims Mike Joyce. Pusey was naturally curious about the subject matter of the opening two lines which hinted at infanticide. As Joyce notes: "The first words were 'In the river the colour of lead, immerse the baby's head'" and it was like 'Stop! What was that you sang?' It was ridiculous. They wouldn't ban a song, just not play it". In fact, the song was broadcast on 21 September 1983.

## YOU'VE GOT EVERYTHING NOW

Although this lacked the organ and piano accompaniment that was later used on the first album, it still sounds surprisingly accomplished. Morrissey's falsetto is again in evidence and the arrangement is consistent with the alternate version.

## ACCEPT YOURSELF

Morrissey's powerful affirmation of individuality is accompanied by an appropriately uneven rhythm. While other songs rage against imagined detractors, here the mood is stoical and the sentiments empowering.

## GIRL AFRAID

It still seems amazing that this song could have been relegated to a mere extra on the rear of the 12-inch version of 'Heaven Knows I'm Miserable Now'. Within the context of 'Hatful Of Hollow', it emerges as a wondrous highlight. Marr's alluring arrangement, originally conceived on piano, provides a perfect counterpoint to Morrissey's morality tale of modern relationships. While it is possible to detect underlying hints of misogyny, the predominant theme is a pervasive, mutual insecurity that gnaws away at the partners and ultimately separates them.

## BACK TO THE OLD HOUSE

Here, Morrissey indulges a sense of loss for something that was never realised. Marr's plangent acoustic work beautifully enhances the mood of empty nostalgia for a relationship that is never described, revealed or requited.

## REEL AROUND
## THE FOUNTAIN

This version was originally slated as a follow-up single to 'Hand In Glove'. It was advertised as such in the music press and several white label copies were pressed which now sell as exorbitantly expensive collectors' items. The attendant controversy over the song's theme and the sudden advent of 'This Charming Man' persuaded Rough Trade to cancel the release. It remains a pleasant addendum to the version featured on the debut album.

## PLEASE PLEASE PLEASE
## LET ME GET WHAT I WANT

This simple expression of hope in the face of constant adversity featured the usual slither of mild irony, a view dependent upon the reading of "Lord knows it would be the first time". Marr adds a plaintive note to Morrissey's pleading with an impressive mandolin solo, all of which takes place within a mere 110 seconds. An impressive ending to a much loved album.

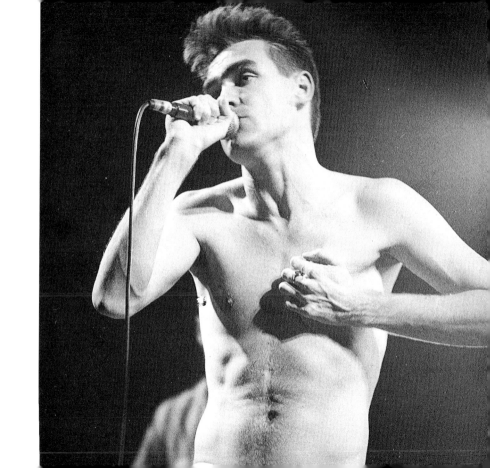

# MEAT IS MURDER

ORIGINAL ISSUE: ROUGH TRADE RECORDS, ROUGH 81, FEBRUARY 1985. REISSUED: ROUGH CD 81 MARCH 1985.
CURRENT ISSUE: WEA 4509-91895-2, NOVEMBER 1993/FEBRUARY 1995.

Following the release of their debut album and the compilation 'Hatful Of Hollow', The Smiths toured extensively and built a sizeable following on the college circuit. Their success in music press polls indicated that they were not merely top of the indie pile but close to making a substantial impact on the pop mainstream. An endearing devotion to the three minute pop single, backed by a formidable songwriting partnership, suggested that they might yet follow previous music press heroes such as The Jam by topping both the singles and albums charts. But it was not to be. For all their awareness of pop history, it seemed The Smiths could not fashion the classic number 1 single that would define their time for ever.

Instead, they were emerging as a striking albums group, buoying their market with quality singles which nevertheless sold in relatively unspectacular quantities. The Smiths would have loved to broadcast their philosophy into the international market with a classic chart topping single, but that was not to be. It would remain the one great flaw in an otherwise glittering career.

The Smiths' impressive ascent since their début album coincided with Morrissey's emergence as pop's most provocative and newsworthy orator. His love/hate relationship with the media saw him lionised in the music press, even while the tabloids called for his head. Although his sexuality and apparent celibacy still fascinated journalists and public alike there was, throughout this period, a discernible shift in emphasis from the personal to the political. Suddenly, Morrisseyspeak was less preoccupied with the monochrome ideals of a lost verdant England and more concerned about contemporary events. His much publicised comments on Margaret Thatcher, British royalty, the IRA, CND, the Brighton Bombing and animal rights heaped controversy on controversy. His views were distilled most forcibly in what was arguably The Smiths' finest album.

'Meat Is Murder' was a thrilling, spinetingling extravaganza with an agenda that both transcended and reflected its time. In Thatcherite Britain, political pop was in vogue and a substantial number of artistes, from the New Pop of Culture Club to the Newer Pop of Frankie Goes To Hollywood and Bronski Beat, were making forthright political statements, usually backed by a sexual agenda. Morrissey was, in many ways, leading the charge, simply by expressing opinions, ideals and prejudices that he had held since troubled adolescence. If 'Meat Is Murder' had been mere sloganeering then it would now be little more than a faintly anachronistic curio. That it was more than that was evident from its musical menu, which was as varied as any listener could desire. The contents offered pop, folk, rockabilly, psychedelia, flashes of funk and even a sprinkling of heavy metal. It was a major step forward from The Smiths' dour first album with a far crisper production, more accomplished musicianship and noticeably improved vocals. The rhythm section received a greater opportunity to explore new ideas, with Rourke introducing funk patterns and Joyce enjoying the freedom to play the way he chose. Marr also found his métier as an arranger/producer

ably assisted by Stephen Street. The strength in unison that the players offered enabled Morrissey to translate his personal neuroses and political pronouncements into a potent body of work that seemed unsurpassable.

## THE HEADMASTER RITUAL

The album opens with one of Marr's greatest and most enticing riffs. The amateurish sound that was evident on several of their earlier recordings has been replaced by a crystal clear production in which every instrument is perfectly balanced. It is clear that Marr paid particular attention to this song which took longer to compose and complete than any other in The Smiths' canon. "I first played the riff to Morrissey when we were working on the demos for our first album with Troy Tate," he told me. "I nailed the rest of it when I moved to Earl's Court. That was around the time when we were being fabulous."

Morrissey's accompanying lyrics spit with the venom of a revenger's tragedy. The victim of his wrath is ostensibly his headmaster at St Mary's, Vincent 'Jet' Morgan. Within the song, however, Morrissey's railing contempt transcends the particular locale and serves as a bitter indictment against all custodial educational institutions. With a less impressive backing, Morrissey's message might have sounded trite and facile but Marr's driving arrangement invests the lyrics with a power and resonance that is truly beguiling.

## RUSHOLME RUFFIANS

The debt that this song owes to Pomus/Shuman's '(Marie's The Name) His Latest Flame' is obvious from a first hearing and Marr would later acknowledge the source in live performance. If the music hinted at plagiarism, then so did the lyrics. Morrissey borrowed freely from the pen of comedienne Victoria Wood and hijacked her song 'Fourteen Again' for his own satiric purposes. What emerges is a striking adaptation in which Wood's humorously affectionate reminiscences are subverted into a threatening landscape where casual violence and the threat of romantic suicide are menacingly present.

With Morrissey and Marr each adapting material from separate sources, both the lyrics and music share a common sense of playful experimentation. As Marr points out, the primary idea was to create a song that captured the raw excitement of youths visiting a Manchester fairground. The rockabilly guitar work gave the song a Fifties' ambience in keeping with the theme. Morrissey also travelled back to his earliest memories in dramatising the dazzling unpredictability of fairground life. "As a child, I was literally educated at fairgrounds," he claimed. "It was the big event. It was why everybody was alive. On threadbare Manchester council estates once a year fairs would come around. It was a period of tremendous violence, hate, distress, high romance and all the truly vital things of life... In Rusholme, it was the only thing people had."

## I WANT THE ONE I CAN'T HAVE

This song takes the form of a series of catchy and amusing epigrams set against a basic chord sequence that came together in the studio surprisingly quickly. As Mike Joyce recalls, "It was just done like a jam and Stephen Street said 'That's great'. We went through it a few times and that was the record. Then Andy put the bass line on."

The track is cleverly placed on the album, neatly interspersed between stronger material, yet contributing to the forward thrust of the music. In concert, the song invariably featured early in the set. During a performance at New York's Beacon Theater, Marr unexpectedly included a few chords of what sounded very much like the chorus of Jimmy Justice's 'When My Little Girl Is Smiling' . 'I Want The One I Can't Have' survived the 'Meat Is Murder' tour and remained in the group's live set until as late as October 1986.

## WHAT SHE SAID

Mike Joyce was given leave to let rip on this song and his forceful drumming ensures its place as one of the hardest rockers in the group's varied canon. As in 'Girl Afraid', Morrissey adopts the persona of a neurotic woman – jobless, loveless, depressed and morbid. Yet there are some wonderful touches of black humour, such as the solace offered by the prospect of a premature death through chain smoking. Blue stocking intellectualism is also placed under serious threat by the emergence of a tattooed boy from the docks of Birkenhead. The scenario has the same comic ambience that Morrissey observed in northern dramas like A Taste Of Honey. And as he once reminded us, "I've never made any secret of the fact that at least 50 per cent of my writing can be blamed on Shelagh Delaney."

## THAT JOKE ISN'T FUNNY ANYMORE

A candidate for the best ever Smiths' song – a view held by both myself and Johnny Marr. The majestic waltz time arrangement and sublime acoustic and electric guitar work culminate in a startling refrain in which Morrissey chants a lament of inexpressible woe. Lyrically, the chorus appears to have been inspired and partly adapted from some lines in the film Alice Adams. While irony is a common device for Morrissey, this is one composition where he appears to have stripped the mask away to reveal his true, unadorned feelings. At least this was the impression he gave when discussing the song. "When I wrote the words for that," he noted, "I was just so completely tired of all the same old journalistic questions and people trying this contest of wit, trying to drag me down and prove that I was a complete fake."

Coming away from the song, however, the feeling conveyed is both that of a quiet desperation and a sense of celebration. As so often happens with The Smiths' work, the music is uplifting to the point where even despair becomes therapeutic.

## HOW SOON IS NOW?

When WEA reissued The Smiths' CD catalogue in November 1993, they followed the American version of the album, which meant a surprise additional track for British listeners. It's somewhat ironic that America which, back in the days of The Beatles, often short changed the public by dropping a couple of tracks from over generous UK releases, should now be the home of the bonus track. Then again, 'How Soon Is Now?' was always the most famous Smiths' song in the USA as a result of Sire using an unauthorised video to promote the work on MTV. Despite considerable efforts to push the song beyond the boundaries of college radio, the all-important chart crossover remained elusive. Even Rough Trade founder Geoff Travis was mystified by its relatively poor sales Stateside. "I can't understand why 'How Soon Is Now?' wasn't a Top 10 single," he told me. "Though perhaps I'm being naïve. If it had broken them in the States, it would have made all the difference."

## NOWHERE FAST

Outrageous humour is the predominant mood of this song, not least because it conjures up an image of Morrissey recklessly dropping his trousers. Reading the lyrics, it almost comes as a surprise to consider the number of images of sterility and artificiality beneath the jokey exterior. Of course, all such considerations are rendered subservient to the overwhelming thrust of the second verse in which Morrissey denounces the monarchy in the cheekiest way imaginable. His lyrics recall numerous outbursts in the press in which he derided the Queen, Princess Diana and the entire royal establishment. The remainder of the song is concerned with the narrator's own spiritual malaise. The sad sound of the train that Morrissey alludes to in the lyrics is echoed in the chugging backing track which drives the song along in rockabilly fashion.

## WELL I WONDER

Here, Marr's delicate acoustic arrangement frames Morrissey's elliptical lyrics which testify to an obsessive fixation with an unnamed object of desire. The theme is reminiscent of 'Back To The Old House' with the narrator not merely musing upon what has been lost but cataloguing the genuine terror of being forgotten.

## BARBARISM BEGINS AT HOME

An excellent album is often made great by the ingenuity of its sequencing and the placing of 'Barbarism Begins At Home' after the slight 'Well I Wonder' is an inspired move. Maudlin introspection amid quiet acoustics is immediately replaced by an unlikely feast of funk in which Rourke revives the spirit of The Freak Party, the ensemble that he and Marr played in a year before the formation of The Smiths. The musical importance of Rourke has frequently been undervalued in profiles of the group, but here his major contribution is self evident. As Mike Joyce enthuses, "The bass line was a killer... It was interesting how Andy got his head around it. When we'd stop he'd continue with a Stanley Clarke bass line. It's incredible how he could shift into that."

In spite of his perennial aversion to dance music, Morrissey loses himself in this seven minute funk excursion, yelping like a recalcitrant puppy as he explores the casual violence of child abuse. 'Barbarism' gives the lie to the

notion that The Smiths were purely one dimensional in their musical approach. At this point in their career they seemed capable of trying anything.

The history of this song in concert is also unusual. It was actually premièred at London's Electric Ballroom on 19 December 1983, a full 14 months before it appeared on album. During the group's performance at the Royal Albert Hall, Dead Or Alive's Pete Burns duetted with Morrissey on the song. It later became a live *tour de force*, sometimes lasting in excess of 15 minutes. In terms of musical influence, it remains Rourke's most significant contribution to the group.

## MEAT IS MURDER

The album's finale opens with the harrowing sounds of the slaughter house, which are used to maximum melodramatic effect. Stephen Street recalls how the song was developed in the studio: "I remember trying to work out how the hell we were going to get those machine noises on 'Meat Is Murder'. We had the good old BBC sound effects records for the cows and sheep but I had to make up some mechanical buzzsaw noises and work out how to do it. I actually came up with the idea of the backwards piano line because Johnny had done some piano and some really menacing things and I was into the idea of turning the tape round. I've always been into backward reverbs..."

Morrissey's proselytising in favour of animal rights is confrontational rather than sentimental. The rhetoric is enhanced by Marr's funereal arrangement while the vocal work is surprisingly compelling. Within the space of a few seconds Morrissey moves from mournful sympathy to righteous indignation. His sloganeering gave animal rights issues prominence in the music press of the period and also affected those in his immediate circle. Both Marr and Joyce became vegetarians as did several others in the group's circle, not to mention a significant proportion of impressionable fans.

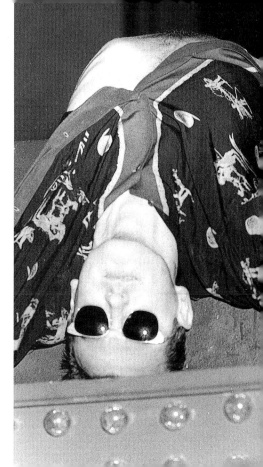

# THE SMITHS

*The Queen Is Dead*

INCLUDES THE SINGLES
**BIGMOUTH STRIKES AGAIN**
+
**THE BOY WITH THE THORN IN HIS SIDE**

# THE QUEEN IS DEAD

ORIGINAL ISSUE: ROUGH TRADE RECORDS, ROUGH CD 96, JUNE 1986.

CURRENT ISSUE: WEA 4509-91896-2, NOVEMBER 1993/FEBRUARY 1995.

The lead up to the release of 'The Queen Is Dead' was a problematic time for The Smiths. They had failed to expand their market sufficiently abroad and, apart from a brief US foray, betrayed a distinct unwillingness to tour outside Britain. At home, their singles sales had declined, with four successive releases failing to crack the Top 20. Worse still, they were beset by financial wrangling, management changes and a dispute with their record company which was threatening to fester into downright war. Extended negotiations over the state of their contract effectively blocked the release of their album for the best part of eight months. In the interim, they suffered a purgatory punctuated by the worrying decline of Andy Rourke into heroin addiction. Following a tour of Eire, he was unceremoniously fired from the group and, almost immediately after, arrested on a charge of unlawful possession of drugs. Then, in a surprise *volte face*, he was reinstated as a Smith. In the meantime, new boy Craig Gannon had been recruited and was kept on as a second guitarist. The sudden changes caused consternation among some fans who felt increasingly that the group was compromising its old ideals and was in danger of losing direction. Others argued the opposite case, pointing to the brilliance of 'Meat Is Murder' and suggesting that the group might equal or even surpass past achievements. In such a climate the new album had much to prove.

Fortunately, 'The Queen Is Dead' turned out to be a masterful work which received excellent reviews and helped the group launch the next stage of their career. The work was later celebrated in various "all time great" critics' polls, even though it failed to secure an album of the year award in the music papers of the period. In 1986 it was seen as a watershed album and over the next 12 months its stature would grow along with The Smiths' reputation.

Looking back, what impresses most about the album is its extraordinary variety of tone. 'Meat Is Murder' had already displayed The Smiths' ability to tackle a wide range of musical styles in an earnest fashion; 'The Queen Is Dead' added a splash of comedy to the mix. Over 10 songs The Smiths shifted from acerbic social commentary to romantic idealism, maudlin despair, misanthropy, light satire, world weary resignation and music hall frivolity. If nothing else, the album exploded the myth of Morrissey as a miserable bastard. Now, even his most myopic critics were forced to acknowledge his pre-eminence as a humorist.

## THE QUEEN IS DEAD

This great epic in The Smiths' canon was Morrissey's most sustained and successful satire on the state of Britain. The stirring Cicely Courtneidge wartime singalong dislocates the time scheme, presenting an image of England which appears to veer between past and present. Despite the song's title, Morrissey's lyrics are playful rather than vicious. There is talk of hanging the Queen but within the dramatic context of the song, Morrissey seeks no more than a brief conversation with Her Majesty after

breaking into the palace. He is, in fact, making a topical allusion here, for the disturbed Michael Fagin achieved precisely that ambition after scaling the palace walls and provoking uproar in the popular press.

Morrissey's satire shifts constantly from the serious to the comic. The allusion to Charles' fantasy transvestism stems from the same self-conscious vulgarity as the trouser dropping incident in 'Nowhere Fast'. As the song progresses, there is a distinct move away from thoughts of regicide to more serious social issues. The state of the monarchy is perceived as one symptom among many for the spiritual decline of England. It is not merely royal decadence, but church materialism, the escapism of the pub and the horrors of pre-adolescence drug addiction that erode the fabric of society. Characteristically, Morrissey fails to resolve the drama but ends the song on a self-reflective note proclaiming his loneliness once more.

Musically, the song is unquestionably one of the group's most impressive and ambitious works. Joyce's forceful opening drum roll and Marr's searing MC5-influenced guitar interplay are breathtaking. As Andy Rourke explains: "'The Queen Is Dead' was done like a jam in the studio. Johnny had this riff and it erupted into this massive wall of sound. It was quite spontaneous." Marr admits that there were some happy accidents that occurred while they were completing the song and these added to its power. "What happened with the feedback," he points out, "was that I was setting my guitar up for the track... I put the guitar on to a stand and it was up really loud... it hit the stand and it made that note of feedback... While we were talking, it was like, 'Wow that sounded good'. So I said, 'Right record that!'" Marr subsequently added a one take solo which left him shaking with excitement.

Stephen Street was equally enthusiastic. "He played blindingly on that track," he recalls. "It was fantastic. In fact, we recorded eight to nine minutes' worth. I had to edit it down. There was more on the 24-track than there is on the mix but we decided that it was a little bit too long so we cut it down." The four man triumph was completed by Rourke with a bass line that Marr claims was "one of his best ever, and something that bass players still haven't matched."

## FRANKLY MR SHANKLY

Industry gossip suggests that the target of this song was Rough Trade founder Geoff Travis. If so, it was camp spite in extremis. For the record, Travis did write poetry, including the tautologically titled "The riff repeats itself over and over again" which was published in his school magazine. As a satire on Morrissey's own role in the pop industry, 'Frankly Mr Shankly' was widely applauded for its ephemeral charm. The actual recording was beset with problems and, as the credits reveal, it was the only track engineered by John Porter. Stephen Street explains: "It was the first time I'd used digital 24 multi-track. We did a great version of that but one day we came in and there was a drop out on the tape so we had to record the whole thing again from start to finish. It wasn't finished when we finished mixing the album. That's why John Porter finished it off."

## I KNOW IT'S OVER

Arguably the bleakest composition in the Morrissey songbook, this remorseless lamentation sounded even more disturbing and jarring following on from the frivolity of 'Frankly Mr Shankly'. 'I Know It's Over' is the cracked mirror image of 'Accept Yourself'; loneliness brings no compensatory strength of independence on this occasion but pure unmitigated despair. Marr finds a suitable accompaniment to the series of suicidal images which reach a maudlin zenith in the refrain which pictures the narrator being buried alive.

## NEVER HAD NO ONE EVER

The funereal mood is retained for this, Morrissey's elegy for a devastated life. A restrained dirge-like accompaniment ends with barely audible sighs and sobs. In the song, life's desperation is said to have lasted exactly 20 years, seven months and 27 days. Applied to Morrissey, who was born on 22 May 1959, this would date his great awakening from depression as 18 January 1980. It would be great to report that something extraordinary happened to him that day but a detailed study of epistolary diaries reveals that all he did was read *The Murderer's Who's Who* and complain about a sore foot. What can I tell you?

## CEMETRY GATES

Morrissey's literary credibility was not seriously affected by his failure to spell cemetery correctly. It was unintentionally ironic that the

error should appear in his most famous song of literary one-upmanship and plagiarism. The ironies multiply when you consider that Morrissey himself indulges in some borrowings during the first verse which bears a striking resemblance to lines uttered by Katharine Hepburn in one of his favourite films *The Man Who Came To Dinner*. Other highlights include the preposterous notion that Wilde is superior to Keats and Yeats combined. For fans there is the added attraction of knowing that the theme of the song alludes to the days when Morrissey visited Manchester's Southern Cemetery, now a regular haunt on Smiths' excursion trips.

On the musical front, Marr again magically finds the perfect arrangement, a light acoustic lilt which improbably emerged when he was trying to compose a song with a Kinks' feel.

## BIGMOUTH STRIKES AGAIN

An alluring acoustic flourish presages Morrissey's politely acerbic vocal on one of the best Smiths tracks of the period. Joyce's speaker splitting drum roll towards the close of the song is absolutely riveting, while Marr adds a relentless rhythm. In those few seconds you understand what the guitarist meant when he described this as the group's 'Jumpin' Jack Flash'. Morrissey's mock martyrdom is also amusingly topical, given his controversial appearances in the tabloids. His vocal is made doubly alluring by the presence of a certain Ann Coates on backing harmonies. As Marr explained, however, this was merely Morrissey's own voice sped up, for the mystery girl was simply a pun on the district Ancoats. With such a powerful record the group must have been confident of securing a sizeable comeback hit single. Amazingly, it only reached number 26.

## THE BOY WITH THE THORN IN HIS SIDE

The minor hit singles of yore continue with this slight but endearing vignette, which preceded the release of 'Bigmouth Strikes Again'. According to Andy Rourke, it was recorded on 16 track at Drone Studios before being remixed by Stephen Street. Although Morrissey reluctantly sanctioned a video to accompany the single, his concession was not rewarded with a massive hit but a disappointing number 23.

Lyrically, this composition is particularly interesting for those fascinated by Morrissey's psychology and willing to accept an autobiographical interpretation. In the song, Morrissey appears to excuse his much publicised hatred by turning inward and diagnosing his condition as resulting from a suppressed desire for love. The switch from singular to plural in the second verse entwines the listener in the drama as the singer urgently seeks empathy. For those who would dare suggest that Morrissey should "get a life" (as Marr later did, incidentally), the song ends by asking the amusingly pertinent questions: how, where and who with?

## VICAR IN A TUTU

Morrissey's saucy tale of a transvestite clergyman was his gentlest satire to date. Typically, the singer ends by directing the humour against himself in the closing line. Real life comparisons between Morrissey and his fabled vicar took a bizarre turn around this time when Ian Pye of the *New Musical Express* was invited to interview the singer at his Kensington home. Upon arrival, Pye reported that he discovered Morrissey dancing wildly around the room, clad in a ballerina's tutu. For one brief moment it seemed that he had become the vicar of his imagination.

Musically, Marr's rockabilly rhythm and Rourke's pleasing bass riff give the song a spontaneous feel. Indeed, Mike Joyce admits that the backing track emerged out of the air one evening when they were limbering up for a session. "We were just playing away in the studio and jamming along," he recalls. "Morrissey would look in and just say 'Carry on'. Around that evolved 'Vicar In A Tutu'. Johnny was just playing a riff and I started playing the drums... If we'd had a name producer I don't think that would have come out. I don't think that would've been the structure of the song."

## THERE IS A LIGHT THAT NEVER GOES OUT

This, Morrissey's great song of romantic adventure, encapsulates his emotional dilemmas in a series of melodramatic musings. There is an incredible lust for life and intense need to escape the shackles of home and family, but no happy ending. Life affirmation soon moves to thoughts of romantic suicide as the narrator pictures a double decker bus hurling himself and his partner into oblivion. The desire to freeze this relationship while it can still be idealised is naturally undercut by the revelation that the romantic dreams are simply fantasy. Much of the humour comes from the extravagant tone and gestures, culminating in the arch reference to something erotic emerging in the darkened underpass. Of course, the relationship is inevitably unrealised as diffidence strangles the possibility of communication, sexual or otherwise.

While the lyrics betray an almost mock romanticism, the song's sentiments are given a sweep of ardent grandeur by the tasteful orchestration. The sleeve credit to the Hated Salford Ensemble suggests that the baton wielder was a familiar figure. "The strings were down to me and the flutes too," confirms Johnny Marr. "The flute part was originally a guitar part."

## SOME GIRLS ARE BIGGER THAN OTHERS

A quiet fade-in introduces Morrissey's satirical comment on the pneumatic wonders of female sexuality. The ribaldry testifies to Morrissey's increasingly irreverent humour and love of comedy. The arrival of *Anthony And Cleopatra* in the narrative owes nothing to Shakespeare but takes its origin from *Carry On Cleo*, in which Sid James is seen cracking open a bottle of ale. For added effect, Morrissey closes the song with a refrain from Johnny Tillotson's 1962 hit 'Send Me The Pillow You Dream On' which sounds as though it has just drifted through the ether to provide a muted conclusion to an extraordinary album.

◇ THE SMITHS THE WORLD WON'T LISTEN

15 TRACKS
INCLUDING
THE HIT SINGLES
'PANIC'
'ASK'
AND
'SHOPLIFTERS OF
THE WORLD UNITE'

ROUGH 101
REMOVABLE STICKER

# THE WORLD WON'T LISTEN

ORIGINAL ISSUE: ROUGH TRADE RECORDS, ROUGH CD 101, MARCH 1987.

CURRENT ISSUE: WEA 4509 91898-2, NOVEMBER 1993, FEBRUARY 1995.

This was 'Hatful of Hollow' revisited and another chance to hear some of The Smiths' rarer material, albeit with something of an over-reliance on the recent success of 'The Queen Is Dead'. The work testified to Morrissey/Marr's continued love of the single format and indicated that a full appreciation of The Smiths required some knowledge of their engaging B-sides and occasional radio sessions. Whatever else 'The World Won't Listen' served its primary purpose by providing casual purchasers with the opportunity to sample the group's work at a more affordable price.

The album arrived at a time when the British music press appeared to be increasingly divided on Smiths' matters. Having previously fallen out and made up with *Sounds* over the paedophile controversy, the group now found new enemies at *Melody Maker*. During the autumn preceding this album's release, an article by Frank Owen was published in which Morrissey was taken to task for his allegedly racist musical views. The controversial single 'Panic' was called "the most explicit denunciation yet of black pop". Morrissey added fuel to the criticism by making insensitive remarks about the state of black music, including the strange and unfounded contention that there was some kind of pro-black conspiracy on *Top Of The Pops*. Not surprisingly, this provoked a stinging attack, followed by a howl of protest from The Smiths' camp. The furore prompted a spate of accusative and defensive letters in the music press. Marr reacted particularly strongly to the allegations and, during a sympathetic interview with the rival *NME*, came on all macho by threatening the *Melody Maker* freelancer with a kick-in. At this stage, the *New Musical Express* had clearly emerged as the most consistent champions of Morrissey/Marr, although they too would fall from favour in later years after questioning the motives of their favourite cover star.

Amid the heated arguments over Morrissey's racial views and the continued relevance of The Smiths, it was no surprise that Britain's two major music publications should find themselves divided about the merits of this latest compilation. Manchester based journalist Dave Haslam gave the work a glowing review in the *NME*. He concluded: "In their finest moments, The Smiths make music that tugs on our memory and gives you great hope." There were no such compliments from *Melody Maker*'s Steve Sutherland, whose antipathy towards Morrissey appeared to be growing with each release. He saw the singer as a cynical opportunist, claiming, "From the Moors Murders scandal early in their career, to the statements supporting the Brighton bombers, to the brief flirtation with the sensual, to the recent reclusive bemused intellectual, it's apparent that Morrissey will stop at nothing to manufacture confrontations with the norm in order that The Smiths remain special... A career in outrage is a fine place to be but some jokes just aren't funny anymore."

Public opinion went with the *NME* camp and the compilation became the third album by the group to reach number 2 in the charts.

# PANIC

With its chorus of "Hang The DJ", this proved one of The Smiths' more controversial songs. Interestingly, there was no problem with radio airplay or hysterical criticism from the popular press. Debate about possible racist connotations in the song seemed restricted to the music weeklies. Marr attempted to defuse the situation by explaining the genesis of the song. It had been written on the day that he and Morrissey heard a news bulletin about the Chernobyl disaster on Radio 1. They were taken aback when this was allegedly followed by Wham's singalong 'I'm Your Man'. Morrissey felt sufficiently indignant about the insensitive radio programming to pen a protest song with the contentious refrain "Hang The DJ". Marr concluded from this that the song was purely a reaction against the superficial tastes of disc jockeys and popular radio programmers.

Of course, 'Panic' was much more than the above. Marr was merely distracting attention from the key refrain "Burn down the disco" which took the debate far outside the boundaries of Broadcasting House and directly on to the dance floor. It was difficult to see how this could be seen as anything other than an attack on the club scene and therein lay much of the problem. That, course, was only part of the story. The chorus aside, the song was, it should be stressed, a spooky comment on urban unrest at a time when memories of inner city rioting were still strong. Derek Jarman's video captured the spirit of the single to great effect and the image of the children chanting the murderous refrain like a dark nursery rhyme was strangely disturbing.

Musically, the distinctive riff owed much to the influence of T Rex's 'Metal Guru'. Both Morrissey and Marr had been keen fans of Marc Bolan during their adolescence so the borrowing was appropriate. Although The Smiths were undertaking an American tour when 'Panic' was released, it gave them a surprise number 11 hit – their third best chart placing.

## ASK

Controversy of a different kind surrounded the hit single 'Ask'. In the wake of Craig Gannon's departure from The Smiths, he brought an action against Morrissey/Marr claiming *inter alia* that he deserved a co-writing credit for the composition. His argument centred on a chord sequence idea that he claimed he'd come up with during the sessions for 'Panic'. Gannon explains: "Me and Johnny were sat in the library playing acoustic guitars and they must have been miked up as we were probably putting down the acoustic tracks for 'Panic'. I just started playing the chord sequence which would later become 'Ask' in exactly the way it appears on the record. Johnny then joined in playing the same... I then forgot about the idea and left it at that".

At a later session, Gannon was surprised to find that the original idea, which he felt was his own, had been developed and was now to be recorded. "Johnny must have played Morrissey this idea or given him the recording I already mentioned. I was completely surprised as we were now recording this for the next single. The only section of the chord structure that I didn't come up with for 'Ask' was the middle eight section with the chords E-minor, D and C. That was actually what Johnny came up with. All the way through the song there is an overdub with me and Johnny sat around a mike with acoustics, playing a riff that he came up with towards the end of the recording of the song. That is a great riff and a real hook but it was still just an overdub and I felt the song was nearly complete without it. Up until the release of 'Ask' I still thought I'd be given a writing credit. When I found that I wasn't given a writing credit, it didn't really bother me, but I thought it was pretty bad that no one even acknowledged that it was my idea in the first place. The thing I hate is that in the past I've been accused of trying to put my name to a song as if I was trying to grab what I could get when that was not the case at all. In any other situation where it would have been up to me to choose to make a song out of such a basic song idea, I probably wouldn't have expanded on that idea, although I do think the song ended up really good."

Marr disagreed with Gannon and felt that his contribution did not merit a co-writing credit. "When he did come up with his own parts, others said it was like something I'd played on the last single," he pointed out. "It wasn't exactly his own style... Craig really threw it away. He really screwed it up for himself." Eventually, the matter was settled out of court and the original song credits remained. Yet another person bothered by the release of 'Ask' was producer John Porter. He remained unimpressed by the final recording, feeling that Morrissey's decision to have the single

remixed thwarted its impact. Recalling the middle section of the song, Porter stresses, "There was this great breakdown with the big wave splashing. It was the most theatrical effect, with seagull noises done by Johnny on the guitar. It was fantastic but, on the record, you don't notice it. It's just gone." The disputes aside, 'Ask' was a sprightly single which justly maintained the group's recent promising run of hits, peaking at number 14.

## LONDON

A tense, driving arrangement characterised this tale of escape from provincial strangulation. The theme owed much to *Billy Liar* and could be regarded as a sequel to 'William, It Was Really Nothing'. The crucial difference is that in Morrissey's scenario the protagonist boards the train and leaves for London, unlike the anti-hero of Waterhouse's novel who abandons his dreams on the station platform.

## BIGMOUTH STRIKES AGAIN

Still recently familiar from its appearance on 'The Queen Is Dead', this unjustly minor hit sounded almost as strong as ever in its new context. Stephen Street had fond memories of the song and with good reason. "I remember that night," he says of the recording. "The session went really well and I asked Johnny and Morrissey whether they'd consider giving me a production point, just one per cent of the sessions that I'd do. They thought about it and said, 'Fine'. So that's how I stepped up from engineer to co-producer."

## SHAKESPEARE'S SISTER

Taking its title from a Virginia Woolf essay, 'Shakespeare's Sister' is an unusually upbeat reflection on the enticing nature of suicide. Morrissey constructs a cliff top drama, throws in a hint of maternal repression, then ends the proceedings on a note of bathos by speculating on his prejudice against acoustic guitars. Stressing what he considered the positive aspects of the composition, and completely ignoring its darker elements, he explained: "The song was really about shrugging off the shackles of depression and shedding the skins of one's parents and getting out and living and doing what one wants to do."

Despite its intriguing literary title, 'Shakespeare's Sister' received a scathing critical response in some quarters and its rela-tive chart failure at number 26 was seen by many as a serious setback for the group. Morrissey rallied to the song's defence but could not stop people questioning the unexpected and sudden decline in the group's popularity as singles specialists. Marr was more stoical about the chart placing, but admitted, "It was a disappointment for me. As a 7-inch single for the group at that point in time, it was quite inventive. There was something about that riff that I always wanted to do. I just flipped all the way whilst we were recording it. I really loved doing it. We didn't get much support from Rough Trade on that one. They didn't like it very much. As with 'Bigmouth' it was a valid 7-inch single to own but maybe not to play on the radio but that's all right by me."

Record plugger Scott Piering did not agree with Marr's contention that the single lacked support. "All they wanted was to have the radio play their records, and they didn't want to give anything back. They wanted to put out lots of singles but some were ill-considered, in retrospect. 'Shakespeare's Sister' was very intense, but it wasn't a radio record. Of course, nobody could tell them what singles were about."

Rough Trade's founder Geoff Travis concurred with Piering's view. "There was a problem with Morrissey thinking he had a divine right to a higher chart position," he noted. "We did as well as anyone in the world could have done with those records".

## THERE IS A LIGHT THAT NEVER GOES OUT

This was the second track on the compilation from the relatively recent 'The Queen Is Dead'. It was intriguing to hear this in a different context from its original setting and it must have been a welcome bonus for purchasers who did not own the former album.

## SHOPLIFTERS OF THE WORLD UNITE

By this point, even Morrissey's titles were getting him into trouble. One tabloid dragged the singer over hot coals for inciting an outbreak of mass shoplifting. It was a ludicrous proposition. Even if the lyrics were taken literally, the possibility of a pandemic union of pilferers would have stretched the credulity of even the most optimistic anarchist. Slightly more interesting than the distracting title was the final

few lines of the song in which Morrissey provides what amounts to an impressive diagnosis of his world weary neurosis ("Tried living in the real world instead of a shell/But I was bored before I even began"). Although 'Shoplifters Of The World Unite' seemed somewhat uncommercial as a single, it climbed to number 12, a position indicative of the group's popularity in early 1987.

## THE BOY WITH THE THORN IN HIS SIDE

Another chance to hear Morrissey stating the validity of his tortured persona. Although this track justified its inclusion on the grounds of its single status, the appearance of a third track from the recent 'The Queen Is Dead' seemed a little overwhelming in the context.

## ASLEEP

With its stark piano accompaniment, this song could have been subtitled 'A Lullaby For Would-Be Suicides'. Unlike Morrissey's other songs of self-destruction there are no deflating, humorous asides here, for the mood is uniformly bleak and the melancholy dangerously alluring. It is alarming to consider that in the wake of The Smiths' demise, there were a small number of reputed suicides. Not that Morrissey has great prospects for the after life. The absolute insistence that there is a better world after death is undermined by the final line in which the narrator clings to the hope that something may be there. The eerie sound of howling wind adds a macabre feel to the song, while the music box version of 'Auld Lang Syne' chillingly tolls out the old world for an uncertain future... *sans* everything.

## UNLOVEABLE

More self-deprecating diffidence from Morrissey and this time he is double tracked at certain points in the song for poignant emphasis. This was previously only available on the 12-inch version of 'Bigmouth Strikes Again'.

## HALF A PERSON

This tribute to obsessive, comic devotion and its effects is arguably The Smiths' finest minor work. Part of its charm comes from the autobiographical associations – for we know that Morrissey visited London when he was 16 years old, a period when he was decidedly clumsy and shy. There is also the additional charm of a possible gender reversal when the protagonist enters the YWCA and attempts to secure a job as a back scrubber. Has Morrissey taken on a female persona here? I would suggest that this is another example of his playful coyness. The deliberately hesitant pause for effect 'Y... WCA' suggests that the singer was about to utter the more likely YMCA. Imagine the eyebrow raising spectacle of Morrissey playing the Village People card with its attendant gay connotations. There is a wonderful pathos in the admission that the singer's whole life can be summed up in this adolescent drama of shyness and solitude. There may also be a tip of the hat to late Fifties pop with the words 'The Story Of My Life' for that title was a number 1 hit for Michael Holliday in 1958.

## STRETCH OUT AND WAIT

This song may be as close as Morrissey ever came to celebrating teenage lust. It is only on keener inspection that you realise that the tortuous philosophical debate advocating the sex act may well be an inhibiting device in itself. The comedy is completed with what sounds like some sighs and mock kisses in the coda.

Source hunters should note that the lines about the world ending were adapted from a scene in the James Dean movie *Rebel Without A Cause*. Although this song was previously issued on the 12-inch of 'Shakespeare's Sister' and a live rendition can be heard on the 12-inch of 'That Joke Isn't Funny Anymore', the version on this collection is an alternate take. It is noticeable that the lyric sheet for this compilation and the later 'Louder Than Bombs' lists the opening line as "Off the high rise estates" rather than the amended "All the lies that you make up" which Morrissey sings.

## THAT JOKE ISN'T FUNNY ANYMORE

The shock of the old as we return to arguably the finest moment on 'Meat Is Murder' and one of The Smiths' all time classics. The new lyric sheet reveals that Morrissey is singing a muted "Why must you kick them when they fall down" which gratified those of us who could not decipher those words which were missing from the transcript of the original album. Speaking of omissions, it should be noted that this is an edited version of the song

cut down for radio play. It fades prematurely, missing out the memorable closing reprise.

## OSCILLATE WILDLY

Marr's attractive tune caught the attention of Geoff Travis who desperately wanted Morrissey to pen a suitable lyric for possible release as a single. Morrissey declined, thereby ushering in the first Marr instrumental. There would be two more later in the group's career including 'Money Changes Everything' which appeared on the cassette version of this compilation.

## YOU JUST HAVEN'T EARNED IT YET BABY

This served as a spiteful riposte against those imagined foes who had held back Morrissey's career by doubting his worthiness. It was originally intended as a single but cancelled in favour of 'Shoplifters Of The World Unite'. Stephen Street remarks, "The one used on the compilation 'The World Won't Listen' was recorded 48-track with John Porter... There were a lot of overdubs and I think they went too far. Morrissey felt that they'd wiped out the feeling of the sog." This was the only previously unreleased song to appear on this compilation, although a number of white label copies had previously been released by mistake in place of 'Shoplifters Of The World Unite'. According to Rough Trade, a clerical error resulted in the wrong stamper being used on several batches of pressings. "Without apportioning blame, there was a mistake at the pressing plant, " the record company insisted. "We only knew about it when a couple of shops rang us."

Morrissey was less than convinced by this explanation and suspected that the white label error may have been a Machiavellian promotions scam. His final words on 'You Just Haven't Earned It Yet Baby' were the curt, "Ultimately, we felt it just wasn't good enough, so it went on the compilation LP." Fortunately, the discerning Kirsty MacColl saw greater value in the song and covered it with considerable aplomb on her 1989 album 'Kite'.

## RUBBER RING

Andy Rourke's prominent bass line introduces Morrissey's plea not to be forgotten by those who once loved his music. It was a fitting conclusion to the album and seen by many as a personal message to those followers already in danger of outgrowing adolescent angst and abandoning Morrissey in adulthood. The song ended with the Oscar Wilde aphorism "Everybody's Clever Nowadays" which also served as a passing nod to The Buzzcocks' 'Everybody's Happy Nowadays'.

# THE SMITHS

"LOUDER THAN BOMBS"

# LOUDER THAN BOMBS

ORIGINAL ISSUE: ROUGH TRADE RECORDS, ROUGH 255/SIRE 9-2569-2, APRIL 1987.

CURRENT ISSUE: WEA 4509-93833-2, NOVEMBER 1993, FEBRUARY 1995.

**W**ith the release of this compilation one month after 'The World Won't Listen' Rough Trade might reasonably be accused of saturating their market. Of the 24 tracks featured, 20 had previously appeared on past albums, while the remaining four were culled from recent 12-inch single releases. In short, there was nothing new here for hard core fans while casual purchasers were offered better value on the aforementioned 'The World Won't Listen'. Rough Trade's suicidal release plan was not without logic. Originally, 'Louder Than Bombs' had been designated solely for US consumption, but the prospect of import copies being sold in the home market at inflated prices persuaded Rough Trade to sanction its UK release.

In retrospect, it is unfortunate that the album was not compiled a little later as it might then have featured the group's final two studio recordings, a cover of Cilla Black's 'Work Is A Four Letter Word' and the George Formby influenced 'I Keep Mine Hidden'. As it stands, Marr was pleased with the double album compilation, feeling that it enabled listeners, particularly in America, to sample a more extensive range of the group's work. "Now I say you can't ignore our singles entity," he stresses. "You have to take 'Louder Than Bombs'. You can't just listen to 'The Queen Is Dead' if you want to know about this group. You have to know our singles philosophy." Marr is quite correct, of course, but not too many people in the UK were entranced by 'Louder Than Bombs' back in 1987. While 'The World Won't Listen' had reached number 2, its unexpected successor barely scraped into the Top 40.

## IS IT REALLY SO STRANGE?

The compilation opens with one of Morrissey's more humorous compositions. Using the old "trip down south" motif, the singer presents us with a hilarious travelogue in which he loses his bag in Newport Pagnell and, amid great confusion, unintentionally kills a horse and a nun. Characteristically violent imagery is used as an expression of commitment, with words such as "kick", "butt" and "break my face" preceding the carefree romantic "'Cause I love you". The tight arrangement enhances the black humour which contrasts markedly with that other runaway song 'London'.

## SHEILA TAKE A BOW

The Smiths go glam rock with a thumping oompah arrangement, straight out of the Gary Glitter school of rock. On closer inspection the melody is reminiscent of David Bowie's 'Kooks', although the tempo is faster. Morrissey's lyrics are a clarion call for teenage rebellion. The song champions the sexual confusion of early Seventies' pop, as narrator and subject swap gender in successive verses. The line "Throw your homework into the fire" was clearly adapted from 'Kooks', wherein Bowie informs his son Zowie, "If the homework brings you down, then we'll throw it on the fire." In common with the T Rex-influenced 'Panic', 'Sheila Take A Bow' reveals

Morrissey and Marr re-creating themselves as Seventies pop idols.

Although the song was originally produced by John Porter, Morrissey appeared to have doubts about its merits and decided to recruit Stephen Street. The song was recut, but nobody bothered to inform Porter who, it turned out, had played a snatch of guitar on the record. When he heard the new version on the radio, he was extremely disenchanted. "The first thing I knew it was out and it sounded slightly different," he recalls. "They had gone in with Stephen Street done the track again, but sampled guitars off the original and put them on this new one without mentioning it to me..." As Porter concludes: "That was the last I ever had to do with The Smiths." His replacement, Stephen Street, stresses that the unauthorised sample was an accident. "With 'Sheila Take A Bow' I never knew until I read *The Severed Alliance* that is was John Porter's playing," he points out. "If I'd known that I'd never have agreed to sample it. I thought it was just a piece of work that Johnny had done and he couldn't be bothered to re-create it. It was a guitar line and sounded good, so why bother doing it again?" Despite all the confusion, the single emerged as a strong, commercial offering which equalled the group's best ever chart placing at number 10.

## SWEET AND TENDER HOOLIGAN

This strident rocker features some engagingly sardonic lyrics from Morrissey on the treatment of violent offenders by liberal juries. The sarcasm is so biting that you are almost left with the impression that the singer is siding with the psychotic "hooligan" who ends the song reciting a funeral oration ("in the midst of life we are in death").

## GOLDEN LIGHTS

With an uncredited Kirsty MacColl on backing vocals, Morrissey tackles Twinkle's endearing vignette on the romantic perils of pop star fame. The unlikely pop godhead mentioned in the song was Bachelors' vocalist Declan McCluskey, who was dating Twinkle at the time. The new recording had a deliberately muted feel which disappointed producer John Porter. "I didn't hear it till it came out," he remembers "and I thought, 'Oh, no!'... We recorded it with these beautiful mandolins and

it sounded fantastic. It had a Mexican feel. The stuff on the tape is beautiful, but the remix sounds appalling to me." Ignoring such niceties, Marr clearly felt the entire song was not worth bothering about and had no place in The Smiths' canon. In his black book, it appears to have been surpassed only by the equally anodyne cover of Cilla Black's 'Work Is A Four Letter Word'.

Full track listing: *Is It Really So Strange?; Sheila Take A Bow; Shoplifters Of The World Unite; Sweet And Tender Hooligan; Half A Person; London; Panic; Girl Afraid; Shakespeare's Sister; William, It Was Really Nothing; You Just Haven't Earned It Yet, Baby; Heaven Knows I'm Miserable Now; Ask; Golden Lights; Oscillate Wildly; These Things Take Time; Rubber Ring; Back To The Old House; Hand In Glove; Stretch Out And Wait; Please Please Please Let Me Get What I Want; This Night Has Opened My Eyes; Unloveable; Asleep.*

# THE SMITHS
## "STRANGEWAYS, HERE WE COME"

# STRANGEWAYS, HERE WE COME

ORIGINAL ISSUE: ROUGH TRADE RECORDS, ROUGH CD 106, SEPTEMBER 1987.

CURRENT ISSUE: WEA 4509-91899-2, NOVEMBER 1993, FEBRUARY 1995.

Following the success of 'The Queen Is Dead', The Smiths were in the ascendant. No longer the private property of the indie circus, they were branching out into mainstream rock with an ever expanding audience. Dogmas already outdated were by now discarded: the group sanctioned videos; announced they were signing to EMI and intended to conquer the USA by playing stadiums. Some fans felt uncomfortable or betrayed by these changes, but others understood that it was an inevitable progression. An eventful 1986 closed with the departure of Gannon, Rourke rehabilitated and Marr almost losing his life in a car crash. The Smiths had come a long way but they were now a stable four-piece again.

1987 seemed certain to be a year of consolidation for a group, now capable of achieving international success. They soon began work on another studio album and, despite some niggling moments, the old camaraderie was still in evidence. Drink flowed freely during the sessions and Marr, in particular, expressed a desire to try out new ideas and explode the crumbling myth of The Smiths as a jingle jangle indie group. In one respect, this seemed a healthy attitude but also testified to underlying problems. Marr was clearly restless and although there was enough interesting music on the new album to satisfy his current needs, he seemed a man in search of fresh challenges.

In the background, The Smiths' perennial business sagas continued to fester. Here, Marr made a firm stand, retaining American manager Ken Friedman, with whom Morrissey had become disenchanted. The decision revealed Marr's increasing independence and suggested that the songwriting partners' magical union was less strong than in times past. The knowledge of Morrissey's jealous tendencies hardly helped matters. He had always resented outside influences on Marr if they were seen as affecting the creative partnership or close personal friendship that had developed over the years.

To make matters more disconcerting, there appeared to be differences of opinion about career objectives. Marr saw the need to seize the moment and transform the group into world beaters with an extensive international tour. Clearly he was tired of The Smiths' penchant for under-achievement. At other times, Morrissey might have agreed to take on the world but in early 1987 he seemed wary of extending his empire and insisted that he did not want The Smiths to become a "mega group". Indeed, he claimed he would much rather just make the records and go home, rather than having to promote the work through interviews and world tours. The extent to which such sentiments were a reaction against Marr's upbeat approach remained an interesting question. One thing already seemed likely: the new album would be the first major Smiths' release not to be accompanied by a full tour.

There was no doubt that the entire concept of The Smiths was now under serious review. Once, Morrissey and Marr had seemed uncannily united in their musical opinions, but Johnny was now growing weary of the old kitsch icons associated with the group. As he told Manchester DJ Dave Haslam: "Towards the end of The Smiths, I realised that the records I was listening to with my friends were more exciting than the records I was listening to with the group. Sometimes it came down to Sly Stone *versus* Herman's Hermits. And I knew which side I was on". Always hip to Manchester's musical undercurrents, Marr surely realised that dance music was on the rise and sooner or later he would be forced into a musical *cul de sac* under The Smiths' banner. He told his fellow players as much, suggesting that they were all in danger of allying themselves to a musical dinosaur. "We're going to end up like The Beach Boys in the blue and white striped shirts," he warned. Marr sensed that rival competitors would eclipse The Smiths if they failed to change their ways... but in what way they should change he seemed not entirely sure.

Those close to The Smiths insist that the breaking point came during an uneasy session in Streatham. As usual, B-sides had to be completed for forthcoming singles releases. Marr suggested that they all deserved a rest after the arduous album sessions, but Morrissey was anxious to complete those commitments forthwith. Under duress, Marr attended the sessions, but he was clearly feeling suffocated by Morrissey's intensity. Probably the last straw was coming to terms with the unedifying material he was forced to work on. 'Work Is A Four Letter Word' and 'I Keep Mine Hidden' revealed Morrissey at his most whimsical, precisely at a time when Marr was most critical of his partner's superficial pop forays.

After completing the sessions, an obviously disillusioned Marr called a group meeting and informed Rourke and Joyce that he was intending to leave The Smiths. They could hardly believe what they heard or face the truth. It wasn't as if Marr could articulate precisely why he wanted to end The Smiths, especially when they still seemed at a creative peak. His reasons seemed myriad: part musical, but also personal. As Rourke suggested to me: "Johnny made it plain that he'd had enough. It had sort of taken over his life, and he wanted out basically. He'd had enough. The demands of Moz he couldn't really handle anymore. Like pandering to his whims. He got sick of all that after awhile." Marr was a little more circum-

spect, adding "The pressure was far too much. I wasn't fed up with the guys, it wasn't that at all. I just felt all of us were in an unhealthy situation and unless we made some moves towards thinking about our future direction, we'd become an anachronism."

For the moment, Marr's direction lay abroad. He flew to Los Angeles, leaving the other Smiths to ponder his next move. At this stage, nobody was entirely sure that Marr would go through with his threats to quit. It was commonly believed that after a period of rest and re-evaluation, he would return to the fold. Morrissey clearly felt this to be the case, but he seems to have seriously misread the depth of his partner's disenchantment. Before long, the group found themselves overtaken by events. The music press had been noticeably tardy in discovering the current crisis in Smithdom, but it was inevitable that rumours would eventually be translated into headlines. Typically, the NME was first with the gossip about a rift and ran a major news story under the arresting title "Smiths To Split". Morrissey denied the rumours, while Rourke and Joyce kept a determinedly low profile. Marr, seemingly convinced that Morrissey had planted the story by some devious means, reacted by confirming that he had indeed left. At least, he saved face by confirming the split himself. In one sense the *NME* rumours had given him the perfect excuse to conclude matters with a clean break and a minimum of psychological games. Any further prevarication or rationalisation was now unnecessary: the cold fact was that Marr would not be returning.

Initially, Morrissey and the others insisted that they would be continuing and undertook a rehearsal with Ivor Perry of Easterhouse. The session proved unproductive, however, and by mid-August Morrissey concluded that it was time to bury The Smiths. He contacted producer Stephen Street and confirmed that he was going solo. The Smiths' demise prompted a flood of elegiac letters to the music press, although a significant number accepted the announcement feeling that it would not be right for them to continue without Marr.

One month later 'Strangeways, Here We Come' was released. The title referred to the Victorian jail in Manchester, already controversial for its over-crowding. As Morrissey said at the time: "The way things are going I wouldn't be surprised if I'm in prison 12 months from now." The album may not have been the group's best record, but in the present climate it was guaranteed a eulogistic welcome. Lyrically, the work seemed dominated by songs about death, almost as if Morrissey was expecting the worst. He had sung of death in the past of course, but never as frequently as this. Ironically, what the album displayed most clearly was a group in the midst of an uneasy, but interesting musical transition. Maybe the next album would have broken the magical spell irrevocably or produced a classic. That, like many other questions, would now never be answered.

## A RUSH AND A PUSH AND THE LAND IS OURS

Morrissey's uneasy relationship with love and death was seldom dealt with more obliquely than in this composition. The narrator announces himself as "the ghost of Troubled Joe", a character hung a year and a half before. The scene then shifts to what appears to be a humorous discussion between an adolescent and his father about the youth's listlessness, followed by morbid speculations on the trials of love. Marr's arrangement sounds different from any other Smiths record, as if he were

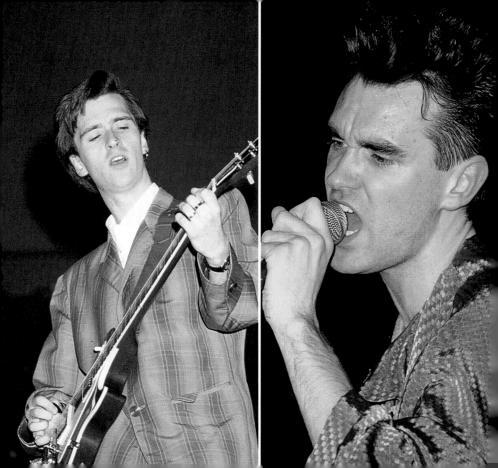

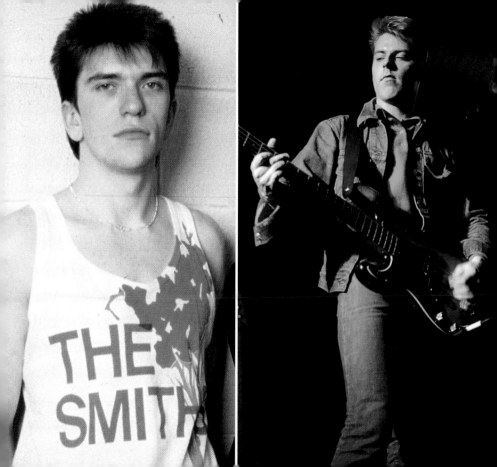

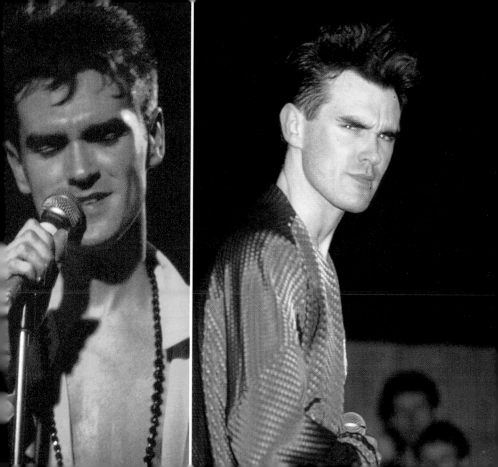

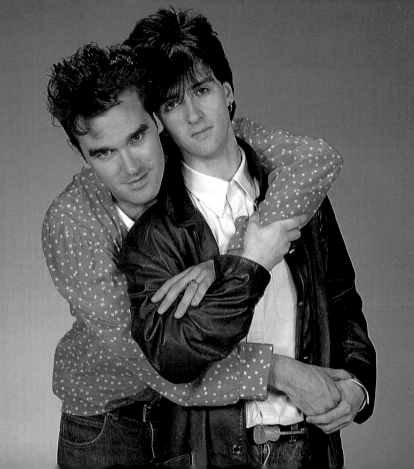

intent on breaking free from the shackles of guitar-based indiedom. As Rourke observed: "'A Rush And A Push And The Land Is Ours' stands out because it didn't have any guitars on it at all. I thought that was a first."

## I STARTED SOMETHING I COULDN'T FINISH

A powerful opening by Marr with a bombastic rhythm brings life to Morrissey's latest romantic saga. The comic understated eroticism is destined never to reveal itself despite Morrissey's sexy attempt at a canine growl. Judging from the lyrics, it's not merely the narrator but the subject of his urges who seems "not too sure" about how to react to a gesture which is deemed "absolutely vile". Although this track was not originally scheduled as a single, it was issued as such and reached a disappointing number 23.

## DEATH OF A DISCO DANCER

This was once compared to the work of Pink Floyd, but a more accurate musical antecedent would be late period Beatles. Marr immerses himself in late Sixties post-psychedelia to con-clude the track with a free-form freak-out in which even the untutored Morrissey is allowed to tinker on the piano. Some critics found the song turgid, but producer Stephen Street was not among them. "I still stand by it being a good track," he insists. "I know it was not liked by many people because it's not as catchy as the other tracks." Lyrically, the song casts a gloomy perspective on the prospects of peace and love. The suggestion that death in discos "happens a lot around here" took on a chillingly prophetic ring several years later when the Manchester club scene was blighted by drug related slayings.

## GIRLFRIEND IN A COMA

After a troubled ghost and dead disco dancer, we next encounter a coma victim. Despite the theme, the mood is jaunty and the song already familiar, having climbed to number 13 during the summer. The narrator's indecision about whether to see the girl is expressed in polite hospital clichés which neatly evoke the emotional confusion amid the drama. There is further comedy in the classic embarrassing utterance, as the singer casually remarks, "there were times when I could have murdered her".

Morrissey's lightness of touch has seldom been bettered.

## STOP ME IF YOU THINK YOU'VE HEARD THIS ONE BEFORE

Morrissey's increasing affection for long song titles exceeded all previous attempts with this dissection of the fag ends of a relationship. The wry lyrics again touch on love and death. Indeed, this is the fourth song out of five on the album to mention death, with an allusion to "the last ten seconds of life" and even thoughts of a mass murder.

Marr literally takes a knife to his guitar strings to provide one of the best and most dramatic openings heard on a Smiths song. He also achieves his ambition of making the group sound fresh and innovative even while they are performing a traditional sounding Smiths song. Morrissey challenges his listeners in a similar way through the deliberately provocative title which virtually invited critics to consider whether he had lapsed into self parody.

This track would have made an excellent single and was intended as such before radio programmers voiced concern over the "mass murder" line. Ostensibly, it was an innocuous enough phrase but, unfortunately, coincided with the recent massacre in Hungerford, during which the deranged Michael Ryan had shot 17 people dead and injured 14 more. In such circumstances, the BBC concluded that the situation was far too sensitive to broadcast the song, so its release as a single was cancelled. Looking back, the decision was understandable, but regrettable. Marr's dramatic closing break would have provided the perfect coda to The Smiths' career.

## LAST NIGHT I DREAMT THAT SOMEBODY LOVED ME

The eerie opening section of this song was adapted from a BBC sound effects recording which Marr had been intending to use elsewhere. "It was basically a different song that Johnny had for the intro," confirms Stephen Street. What sounds like a trip through Dante's Hell, or a journalist's nightmarish encounter with the brutality of the miners' strike, serves as a dramatic introduction to Morrissey's woeful lament. Once again, the theme concerns the absolute hopelessness of finding love. In the final two lines, Morrissey reiterates the sentiments of 'Stop Me If You Think You've Heard This One Before', fully aware that he is sounding like a worn out record but insistent that the story must go on. His love lorn persona may be predictable but the aching vocal is still moving, perhaps more so due to Marr's expressive "Orchestrazia Ardwick" arrangement.

## UNHAPPY BIRTHDAY

Marr's enticing acoustic arrangement provides a contrasting complement to Morrissey's politely sung but spiteful lyrics. Although the rhythm is upbeat, Marr detected signs of a melancholy lilt buried beneath. As he told me: "There's an air of foreboding that's definitely there in that track 'Unhappy Birthday'." Again, images of death dominate the narrative. Having previously alluded to the killing of a horse in 'Is It Really So Strange?' pop's premier animal rights' lover this time threatens to kill a dog. The song concludes with the narrator shooting himself in a fit of romantic bitterness.

## PAINT A VULGAR PICTURE

With its Wildean title and bitter indictment of record company exploitation it was unsurprising that many interpreted this as an attack on Rough Trade. In particular the lines "Reissue! Repackage!" took on an eyebrow raising significance when applied to the recent flurry of Rough Trade compilations. Add to that the repeated use of one of Geoff Travis's phrases 'You Just Haven't Earned It Yet Baby' and the battle lines seemed clearly drawn. Morrissey denied the connection but it is difficult to believe that he was unaware of the connotations of the song. Of course, he had no good cause for castigating his record company's marketing, for he had sanctioned the compilations himself and was therefore equally responsible for foisting them on the public.

There has also been some fruitless speculation on the identity of the dead star apotheosised in the song, with Morrissey's idol Billy Fury being an all too obvious suggestion. The lyrics, however, give the lie to such a view. Fury's death did not unleash a record company feast of exploitative releases and he had nothing to do with radio A-lists, world tours or MTV, as mentioned in the song. The lyrics are far more appropriate to modern day stars and Morrissey may well have been musing on the after effects of his own death while composing the lyrics.

The twin theme of the song is actually the relationship between star and fan. Morrissey captures the ambivalence of the obsessive star worshipper whose crowning moment was actually touching his object of devotion at a soundcheck and suffering not brutal rejection but a complete lack of acknowledgement and empathy. Ironically, death not only brings cheer to the rapacious record company but also enshrines the star's immortality for the sad fan.

## DEATH AT ONE'S ELBOW

The title was borrowed from the Orton diaries and, judging from the lyrics, so was the theme. Joe Orton was killed by his homosexual companion with a hammer but Morrissey prefers a hatchet. In his scenario, it is the assailant who seems likely to die in a suicide pact, complete with the refrain of The Searchers' 'Goodbye My Love' in the background. Marr's harmonica work, reinforced by a rockabilly style arrangement adds an incongruously sprightly feel. This was the seventh death-related song on the album, which is excessive even by Morrissey's morbid standards.

## I WON'T SHARE YOU

A poignant if understated conclusion to the album which fades out with the forlorn singer reminding himself "This is my time". Inevitably, the title provoked speculation about the identity of the narrator's object of jealous affection, not least among some of The Smiths. "I always got the impression that was obviously about Johnny," Andy Rourke suggests. "Who he wouldn't share him with, I don't know!"

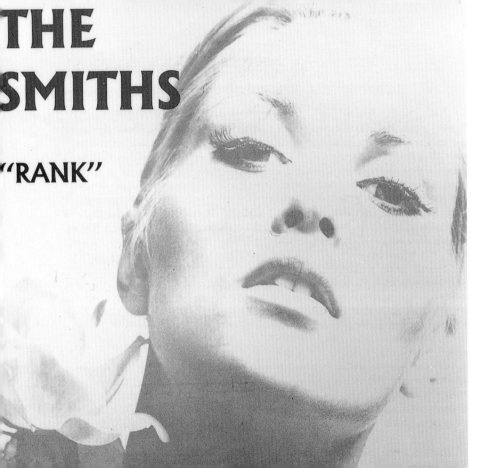

# RANK

ORIGINAL ISSUE: ROUGH TRADE RECORDS, ROUGH CD 126, SEPTEMBER 1988.

CURRENT ISSUE: WEA 4509-91900, NOVEMBER 1993, FEBRUARY 1995.

One year after the release of their final studio album, this posthumous live set was issued and rapidly climbed to number two in the charts. The Smiths could have chosen almost any phase of their career and conjured a live set of interest but, not unexpectedly, they chose a date from their final tour. This was a time when the group were at their rocking best, with a full five piece line up hardened by an arduous American tour. However, it was also a troublesome period in which live gigs took on a more menacing aspect. Cumulative success had brought larger audiences, whose constituency not only included indie fans and college students, but a sizeable spattering of hard rock fans. Although the group's followers were well used to packed halls and sandwiched bodies, they were less enamoured of this macho and often brutal element. Spitting, jostling, punching and near rioting were now more representative of Smiths' concerts than gladioli, National Health spectacles or loving embraces.

The tour was beset by dramatic events, and a series of worrying injuries. In Newport, Morrissey was dragged from the stage, struck his head on the floor and was forced to retire hurt. When sound engineer Grant Showbiz announced the news of the singer's departure to the angry audience, he was struck by a flying bottle, then taken to hospital to be treated for cuts and concussion. Police arrived on the scene to prevent further ugly outbreaks and afterwards several complaining letters to the music press castigated Morrissey for not being a trouper and coming back on. Nor was this gig an isolated incident. In Preston, one week later, The Smiths played the shortest set in their history, when the evening came to a dramatic close after just one song. Morrissey suffered another injury, this time from a flying missile which was later identified as a drum stick. The fact that the opening song was 'The Queen Is Dead' encouraged Marr to spout the implausible suggestion that the group were the recipients of violence from a bunch of pro-royalists!

It was between these two riotous gigs that 'Rank' was recorded at the National Ballroom, Kilburn, on 23 October. It was an eventful evening for all concerned, not least the support group, Soil. Their drummer Gary Farrell, a former pupil of Morrissey's hated school St Mary's, had once turned down the chance to join The Smiths. Now, four years on, he was playing with them on the same bill. The newly scarred Grant Showbiz could also look fondly back at the live recording, for it brought him a much deserved 1% royalty which turned out to be an unexpected financial windfall.

The Smiths played 21 songs that night, 14 of which were extracted for inclusion on 'Rank'. There must have been some temptation to include the entire concert on a double set, but Rough Trade restricted themselves to a single album comprising 56 minutes of music. Few customers would deny that they had got a bargain. Completists were left to track down the original bootleg concert tape which featured the additional 'I Want The One I Can't Have', 'There Is A Light That Never Goes Out', 'Shakespeare's Sister', 'Frankly Mr Shankly', 'Never Had No One Ever', 'Meat Is Murder' and 'How Soon Is Now?' There was even some small consolation for those Mancunians unable to make the trip to London for the big show. That same evening, Morrissey was featured on Tony Wilson's regional arts programme *The Other Side Of Midnight* reviewing Norman Tebbitt's autobiography. His scabrous comments were not available to southern audiences.

The Kilburn gig could not have come at a more crucial or eventful time. Within a week, the unfortunate Craig Gannon was ousted from the group in the most regrettable and casual way imaginable. Two weeks later, Marr was involved in a car crash from which he was, in Mike Joyce's words, "very lucky to keep his legs". This almost James Dean-like conclusion to The Smiths' saga turned out to be part of the closing act. Marr went to hospital the following day where he was fitted with a neck brace and splints. A gig shortly afterwards for the Anti-Apartheid organisation was understandably rescheduled for December at the Brixton Academy. That turned out to be the last ever gig played by The Smiths on British soil. After just over four years of performance the dream was over. 'Rank' served as a belated and much treasured memento of a turbulent period.

## THE QUEEN IS DEAD

The Philadelphia Orchestra's version of Prokofiev's *Romeo And Juliet* provides the perfect dramatic opening to this live album. The classical refrain brings an enormous sense of expectancy, complemented by the swirling lights which announce the imminent arrival of the group on stage. Then suddenly, they are there. A raucous "Hello" precedes some powerhouse drumming before Marr emerges with what is undoubtedly the *tour de force* of the entire set. The song is taken at a furious pace as Johnny wah-wahs into the stratosphere backed by some sterling work by Gannon and Rourke. Morrissey is left almost breathless at times as he tries to keep up with the players. For tricky word endings he substitutes guttural noises and almost sings in tongues during the word "castration". For The Smiths to open a show with an epochal track like this displayed an extraordinary confidence and gave notice that they were intent on rocking out, perhaps like never before.

## PANIC

A long drum solo kicks off the song that restored their Top 20 chart placing. There is little the group can do to compensate for the loss of the child choir in the final verse and throughout the song Morrissey sounds in urgent need of vocal accompaniment. Instrumentally, there are no cracks to paper over. The addition of Gannon gives Marr the necessary space to fatten the sound and he closes proceedings with another spacey flourish.

## VICAR IN A TUTU

This faster paced version offers some amusing vocal dexterity from Morrissey while the group sound like they are enjoying the comic romp. Not surprisingly, this live set featured a high proportion of songs from the still recent 'The Queen Is Dead'.

## ASK

"This is our new single," says Morrissey, before growling, "'Ask'." The performance is very tight and sounds impressively like the recorded version. Marr and Gannon combine their guitar work which meshes well in this obviously well rehearsed number. Morrissey appears to make a special effort in enunciating the hard northern "a" sound for emphatic effect. The song still surprises with its casual sting in the tail line about "the Bomb" achieving what love cannot by bringing the protagonists together.

## RUSHOLME RUFFIANS

Morrissey and Marr mischievously acknowledge this song's debt to Elvis Presley's '(Marie's The Name) His Latest Flame' by incorporating its first verse as an amusing introduction. It is worth noting that the inspiration for 'Rusholme Ruffians' emerged after Marr had been listening to his parents' copy of the Pomus/Shuman classic. "I loved 'His Latest Flame'," Marr admits. "But from being a kid I noticed how many other songs had that chord change. When Morrissey sang it, it sounded really brilliant."

The segue into 'Rusholme Ruffians' is expertly done, with Marr suddenly shifting gear and speeding up the song, much to the audience's appreciation.

## THE BOY WITH THE THORN IN HIS SIDE

Another impressive guitar opening reveals Marr and Gannon working well together. Morrissey's vocal is very confident, complete with a growl or two and the customary falsetto.

## WHAT SHE SAID

A Morrissey belch launches the group into a fiercely driving version of this song from 'Meat Is Murder'. The tempo is slightly slower than the studio version, but the real surprise comes with the additional outro from 'Rubber Ring' which is tagged on at the end and works extremely well.

## IS IT REALLY SO STRANGE?

A polite introduction is followed by another belch as Morrissey canters through this tale of his zany journey around England. It's intriguing to hear the way he pronounces Newport Pagnell and rolls the "r" sounds around his tongue as if he's practising for a French oral exam.

## CEMETRY GATES

At first blush this is far less impressive live than might have been expected. The charm of the album version is missing despite Morrissey attempting to invest some verve into the song by pointedly growling "some dizzy whore." Marr's little false ending is a pleasant touch, but the delicacy of the original is somewhat lost in translation.

## LONDON

By contrast, 'London' works extremely well as the group are given freedom to rock out. What emerges is an unexpected highlight with Morrissey dragging out the syllables to add some new drama to the proceedings. Joyce flails away mercilessly at the end for the obligatory emphatic ending.

## I KNOW IT'S OVER

When Morrissey sings about death by rivers and razors you can't help wondering whether he has been reading Dorothy Parker's *Résumé*. What's missing is any sign of his sardonic humour as a grim, despairingly claustrophobic mood overwhelms him like the funeral soil he describes. This version builds up to an impressive climax, lasting in excess of seven minutes. It serves as the morbid centrepiece to the live album.

## THE DRAIZE TRAIN

This instrumental, previously premiered on single only, serves as an opportunity to focus attention on the players. Its inclusion was fortuitous for Marr, who ended up getting a slightly larger share of the album's publishing than his partner. This was the track that Geoff Travis and others felt should have been issued as a single with some suitable Morrissey lyrics. Despite various solicitations, however, the singer was unimpressed and declined to pen a single word. As Marr admitted, "That was his feeling, yes, and there was strong pressure on him from Rough Trade. It could have been really good but it became a matter of principle with him. He felt the way he did. It didn't click with him. Simple as that, really."

## STILL ILL

This was the oldest song in the live set and the only representative from the group's début album. It's clear how much Morrissey's voice has changed over the years. As if aware of this, he plays with the lines, looking back with comic affection at his younger self. This time when he ponders the "Does the body rule the mind...?" conundrum, he screams "I dunno" loudly, as if tired of all the cod philosophical speculation.

## BIGMOUTH STRIKES AGAIN

This, the final encore, offers a less arresting finale than we might have expected. Marr, for once, seems incapable of reproducing the studio guitar sound to spectacular effect. Even Gannon's presence does not compensate and Marr could really do with a third guitarist here. Fortunately, Morrissey plays up the drama of the song to maximum effect with an endearing range of gargles, grunts and vocal pyrotechnics. The tapes continue to roll after The Smiths leave the stage and it is a nice closing touch to hear the frustrated handclaps and nostalgic echo of Shirley Bassey's 'You'll Never Walk Alone'. Those final moments, along with the dramatic Prokofiev opening, take you back to the concerts of 1986 as much as the songs contained herein. A fine memento.

# BEST... 1

ORIGINAL ISSUE: WEA 4509-90327-2

The first retrospection offered by WEA following their acquisition of The Smiths' catalogue was something of an anti-climax, although its chart performance exceeded expectations. Released at a time when Morrissey's younger audience was ready to reinvestigate The Smiths' back catalogue, it had its place, but the decision to stagger the Best Of concept over two albums seemed nothing less than cheap and exploitative. What could have been a great album sounded little more than a superior sampler.

Full track listing: *This Charming Man; William, It Was Really Nothing; What Difference Does It Make?; Stop Me If You Think You've Heard This One Before; Girlfriend In A Coma; Half A Person; Rubber Ring; How Soon Is Now?; Hand In Glove; Shoplifters Of The World Unite; Sheila Take A Bow; Some Girls Are Bigger Than Others; Panic; Please Please Please Let Me Get What I Want.*

# BEST... 2

ORIGINAL ISSUE: WEA 4509-90406-2

Even The Smiths' faithful following gave this compilation the cold shoulder and it barely succeeded in denting the album charts. Essentially a mopping up exercise after the first Best Of, its target audience appeared to be those hard done by collectors who might buy anything in a new sleeve. The haste and lack of thought that seemed to accompany these compilations made you wonder what WEA might foist upon the public next. Fortunately, their marketing zeal cooled and the next compilation would prove a more dignified and welcome collection.

Full track listing: *The Boy With The Thorn In His Side; The Headmaster Ritual; Heaven Knows I'm Miserable Now; Ask; Oscillate Wildly; Nowhere Fast; Still Ill; Bigmouth Strikes Again; That Joke Isn't Funny Anymore; Shakespeare's Sister; Girl Afraid; Reel Around The Fountain; Last Night I Dreamt That Somebody Loved Me; There Is A Light That Never Goes Out.*

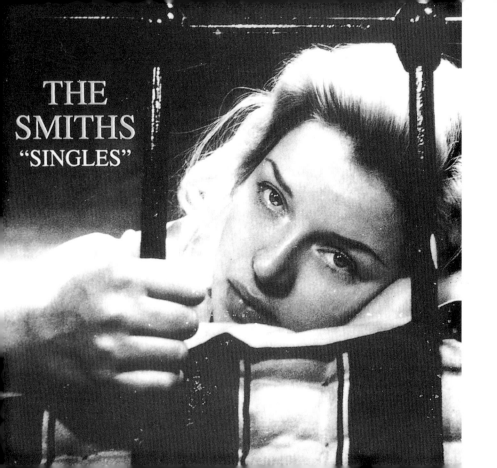

# THE SMITHS
## "SINGLES"

# SINGLES

ORIGINAL/CURRENT ISSUE: WEA 4509-99090-2, FEBRUARY 1995.

Although obviously offering nothing previously unavailable on album, this compilation of The Smiths' singles was a welcome and overdue addition to their catalogue. It immediately made the previous "Best Ofs" not merely redundant but unnecessary and made you wonder why Warners hadn't released this record in the first place. Five star reviews abounded, reminding us once again how much The Smiths continue to be respected by the music press. A first class record.

Full track listing: *Hand In Glove; This Charming Man; What Difference Does It Make?; Heaven Knows I'm Miserable Now; William, It Was Really Nothing; How Soon Is Now?; Shakespeare's Sister; That Joke Isn't Funny Anymore; The Boy With The Thorn In His Side; Bigmouth Strikes Again; Panic; Ask; Shoplifters Of The World Unite; Sheila Take A Bow; Girlfriend In A Coma; I Started Something I Couldn't Finish; Last Night I Dreamt That Somebody Loved Me; There Is A Light That Never Goes Out.*

# smiths singles

The Smiths always placed great pride in their singles work, carefully ordering releases that featured a healthy selection of material unavailable on album. Over the years, most of these tracks have been issued on CD compilations, most notably 'Hatful Of Hollow', 'The World Won't Listen' and 'Louder Than Bombs'. However, as the below singles discography indicates, several live tracks, remixes and a handful of songs remain available on single vinyl or cassette format only. These include 'Jeane'. 'Wonderful Woman', 'Money Changes Everything', 'The Draize Train' (studio version), 'Work Is A Four Letter Word', 'I Keep Mine Hidden' and 'What's The World' (cassette issue). At present there are no plans for these tracks to be issued on CD but they may become available on a compilation or boxed set some time in the future.

## 7-inch singles

Hand In Glove/Handsome Devil (live)
*RT 131 May 1983*

This Charming Man/Jeane
*RT 136 November 1983 (A limited number of test pressings of the cancelled 'Reel Around The Fountain'/'Jeane' are in existence.)*

What Difference Does It Make?/Back To The Old House
*RT 146 January 1984 (During February 1984 a limited number of DJ-only promotional copies of 'Still Ill'/'You've Got Everything Now' [R61 DJ] were circulated in order to plug the group's début album.)*

Heaven Knows I'm Miserable Now/ Suffer Little Children
*RT 156 May 1984*

William, It Was Really Nothing/Please Please Please Let Me Get What I Want
*RT 166 August 1984*

How Soon Is Now?/Well I Wonder
*RT 176 February 1985*

Shakespeare's Sister/What She Said
*RT 181 March 1985*

That Joke Isn't Funny Anymore/Meat Is Murder (Live)
*RT 186 July 1985*

The Boy With The Thorn In His Side/ Asleep
*RT 191 September 1985*

Bigmouth Strikes Again/Money Changes Everything
*RT 192 May 1986*

Panic/Vicar In A Tutu
*RT 193 July 1986*

Ask/Cemetry Gates
*RT 194 October 1986*

Shoplifters Of The World Unite/Half A Person
*RT 195 January 1987*

Sheila Take A Bow/Is It Really So Strange?
*RT 196 April 1987*

Girlfriend In A Coma/Work Is A Four Letter Word
*RT 197 July 1987*

I Started Something I Couldn't Finish/ Pretty Girls Make Graves
*RT 198 October 1987*

Last Night I Dreamt That Somebody Loved Me/Rusholme Ruffians
*RT 200 December 1987*

This Charming Man/Jeane
*WEA YZ 0001 August 1992*

How Soon Is Now?/Hand In Glove
*WEA YZ 0002 September 1992*

There Is A Light That Never Goes Out/ Hand In Glove
*WEA YZ 0003 December 1992*

Ask/Cemetry Gates
*WEA YZ 0004 February 1995*

# 12-inch & cd singles

This Charming Man (Manchester)/ This Charming Man (London)/Accept Yourself/ Wonderful Woman
*RTT 136 November 1983*

This Charming Man (New York Mix – Vocal)/This Charming Man (New York Mix – Instrumental)
*RTT 136 December 1983*

What Difference Does It Make?/Back To The Old House/These Things Take Time
*RTT 146 February 1984*

Heaven Knows I'm Miserable Now/Suffer Little Children/Girl Afraid
*RTT 156 May 1984*

William, It Was Really Nothing/Please Please Please Let Me Get What I Want/How Soon Is Now?
*RTT 166 August 1984*

Barbarism Begins At Home/Barbarism Begins At Home
*RTT 171 January 1985 (A promotion only release in a limited edition of 500 copies)*

How Soon Is Now?/Well I Wonder/Oscillate Wildly
*RTT 176 February 1985*

Shakespeare's Sister/What She Said/Stretch Out And Wait
*RTT 181 March 1985*

That Joke Isn't Funny Anymore/ Nowhere Fast (Live)/Stretch Out And Wait (Live)/Shakespeare's Sister (Live)/Meat Is Murder (Live)
*RTT 186 July 1985*

The Boy With The Thorn In His Side/Asleep/Rubber Ring
*RTT 191 September 1985*

Bigmouth Strikes Again/Money Changes Everything/Unloveable
*RTT 192 May 1986*

Panic/Vicar In A Tutu/The Draize Train
*RTT 193 July 1986*

Ask/Cemetry Gates/Golden Lights
*RTT 194 October 1986*

Shoplifters Of The World Unite/Half A Person/London
*RTT 195 January 1987 (Initial versions of 'Shoplifters Of The World Unite' were despatched with 'You Just Haven't Earned It Yet, Baby' on the A-side)*

Sheila Take A Bow/Is It Really So Strange?/Sweet And Tender Hooligan
*RTT 196 April 1987*

Girlfriend In A Coma/Work Is A Four Letter Word/I Keep Mine Hidden
*RTT 197 July 1987*

I Started Something I Couldn't Finish/Pretty Girls Make Graves/Some Girls Are Bigger Than Others
*RTT 198 October 1987 (Cassette versions of the single included a cover version of James' 'What's The World?', recorded live in Glasgow)*

Last Night I Dreamt That Somebody Loved Me/Rusholme Ruffians/Nowhere Fast
*RTT 200 December 1987 (The CD version of this single featured an extra track: 'William, It Was Really Nothing')*

Barbarism Begins At Home/ Shakespeare's Sister/Stretch Out And Wait
*RTT 171 CD November 1988*

The Headmaster Ritual/Nowhere Fast (Live); Stretch Out And Wait (Live)/ Meat Is Murder (Live)
*RTT 215 CD November 1988*

This Charming Man (Manchester Mix)/ Jeane/Wonderful Woman/ Accept Yourself
*YZ 0001 CD1 August 1992*

This Charming Man (Manchester Mix)/This Charming Man (London Mix)/This Charming Man (New York Mix)/This Charming Man (New York Instrumental)/This Charming Man (Peel Session)/This Charming Man (Single Remix)/This Charming Man (Original Single Version)
*YZ 0001 CD2 August 1992*

How Soon Is Now? (edit)/The Queen Is Dead/ Handsome Devil/I Started Something I Couldn't Finish
*YZ 0002 CD1 September 1992*

I Know It's Over/Suffer Little Children/Back To The Old House/How Soon Is Now? (Album Version)
*YZ 0002 CD1 September 1992*

There Is A Light That Never Goes Out/Hand In Glove (Live)/Some Girls Are Bigger Than Others (Live)/Money Changes Everything
*YZ 0003 CD1 December 1992*

There Is A Light That Never Goes Out/Hand In Glove (featuring Sandie Shaw)/I Don't Owe You Anything (featuring Sandie Shaw)/Jeane (featuring Sandie Shaw)
*YZ 0003 CD2 December 1992*

Ask/Cemetry Gates/Golden Lights
*YZ 0004 CD1 February 1995*

*EP The Peel Sessions*. What Difference Does It Make?/Miserable Lie/Reel Around The Fountain/Handsome Devil
*Strange Fruit SF PS 055*

In addition to the above, The Smiths have appeared on various samplers, imports and rare special promotion discs and test pressings. Rough Trade retrospectively issued several of The Smiths' 12-inch singles on CD. Strangely, the transference from vinyl to CD single was never completed, most of the rarer items remained on vinyl and the ordering of releases was neither chronological nor logical. Those back catalogue singles that did emerge on Rough Trade CD included 'What Difference Does It Make?', 'William, It Was Really Nothing', 'The Boy With The Thorn In His Side', 'Panic', 'Ask' and 'Last Night I Dreamt That Somebody Loved Me'. Catalogue numbers were the same as the Rough Trade 12-inch releases, with the suffix "CD". Singles were repackaged in various countries, occasionally with edited versions, but the only alternate take of which I am aware is the Italian version of 'How Soon Is Now?' on the flip side of the 12-inch 'William, It Was Really Nothing' (Italy: Virgin VINX 71). On 25 May 1984, the *New Musical Express* issued a free EP (GIV 1) featuring 'What She Said'. At one point, a live EP was rumoured for release featuring 'Meat Is Murder', 'Nowhere Fast', 'What She Said', 'Stretch Out And Wait', 'William, It Was Really Nothing' and 'Miserable Lie'. The tracks later appeared on various 7-inch and 12-inch B-sides. A live version of 'Girl Afraid' was also available, by mail order only, on the *NME* Various Artistes compilation 'Department Of Enjoyment'.

# MORRISSEY

*"Viva Hate"*

# morrissey albums
## VIVA HATE

ORIGINAL/CURRENT ISSUE: HMV CDCSD 3787, MARCH 1988.

**T**he most extraordinary aspect of 'Viva Hate' was the speed with which it was completed and released. After the dramatic break-up of The Smiths, one might have expected Morrissey to fall into a despondent gloom resulting in stasis. Instead he responded to the challenge of a new solo career with an alertness and confidence which was most surprising.

After writing to Stephen Street during August and announcing his intentions to complete a new album, the two spent the early winter at the Wool Hall in Bath working with apparent ease on new material. Street brought in Durutti Column guitarist Vini Reilly, whom he had previously worked with and, despite some aesthetic disagreements in the studio, there was much to recommend the partnership. Reilly was another Mancunian of Irish stock and his world view would have appealed to Morrissey. A creature of mood, Reilly could relate to Morrissey's forthright attitude without pandering to his whims. The guitarist's frailty, exacerbated by an eating disorder that

precluded touring, meant that Morrissey was dealing with someone whose problems outweighed his own. Both were essentially outsiders, working in a music business which enabled them to transform their neuroses into an art all the more striking because of its painful roots. Reilly's non-rock pedigree ensured that he could work with Morrissey without being overwhelmed by The Smiths' myth. Inevitably, there would be comparisons with Marr, but Reilly was such a 'strikingly different guitarist that these proved irrelevant.

The burden of composing the songs did not fall on Reilly who, by his own admission, lacked the pop sensibility that Morrissey required. It was Stephen Street who had the unenviable task of providing the melodies that would launch Morrissey on the hazardous road to solo success. Street was not a known song-smith and Morrissey took a considerable risk working with somebody whose pedigree was largely untested. Not for the first time, Morrissey saw something in a partnership that others might have cautioned against. It was partly the security of familiarity for, over the years, Morrissey had worked closely with Street as both engineer and producer and clearly admired his work. He also heard some-thing in the demos that Street posted to him that sounded commercial yet interesting enough to be allied to his lyrics. Perhaps more importantly it seemed a relatively painless way to break the Marr spell.

The general critical reaction to 'Viva Hate' was warm surprise. It followed on so quickly from The Smiths that the reverential attitude towards Morrissey had yet to cool. The album was not an outright classic and occasionally sounded leaden in places but there was an exuberance of discovery there that was at times irresistible. As it turned out, Street's greatest forte was in the area that The Smiths

most prized – the ability to write a strong sin-gle. Both 'Suedehead' and 'Everyday Is Like Sunday' were class records that brought Morrissey his greatest chart success. It seems odd to consider that Morrissey was a hot tip to register a number 1 single at this time but, as it transpired, the early Street era represented his commercial peak as far as *Top Of The Pops* was concerned. He may have recorded better material but has never looked quite such a happening singles artiste since this exciting early run. But 'Viva Hate' wasn't just about singles success. The album also reached number 1, equalling the achieve-ment of 'Meat Is Murder' and suggesting that Morrissey was poised for a formidable albums career at will. Few could have predicted what would happen next.

## ALSATIAN COUSIN

Morrissey opens his solo album with a sound more in keeping with an ambient-tinged heavy metal group on the rampage. Reilly's distorted guitar and Paresi's booming drums take us as far away from the familiar Smiths' sound as possible. The lyrics betray a prurient, almost voyeuristic, character as Morrissey finds eroticism in quizzing his subject about whether or not sex has taken place. Such questions might be transferred back to the singer, which is part of the song's appeal. It is instructive to compare the original demo of the song that Street played to me with the final version. As Vini Reilly noted, "Stephen Street had a cyclical, repetitious bass line and a drum machine. That was the demo – just a bass riff. It didn't really change." Reilly recalls doing some wild jamming on the track, which appealed to Morrissey. "I know Morrissey thinks it's vaguely interesting," Vini remarks. "That was very satisfying because I freaked out on it and it was very radical. I got a really distorted guitar sound with the help of Stephen Street, who's a first class engineer. Praise where it's due - he's a brilliant engineer. So the guitar sound I wanted he was able to get for me with over the top distortion. That one I really enjoyed."

Street adds some memories of his own: "I played it to the guys and they fell about laughing because is was as basic as you've heard it – just a drum machine and a bass line in it. I said 'I want you to leave it open so you can just go mad over the top of it'. It so happened that Morrissey was doing his high, wavering stuff, high yelps and I gave Vini a free hand and he did a great job on it. The beginning I really liked. Andrew's drums worked very well and Vini added to the chords that I'd originally written. He added some harmonies to it. It was nice and solid."

## LITTLE MAN, WHAT NOW?

Morrissey's penchant for borrowed titles continues. 'Alsatian Cousin' came from Alan Bennett's play *Forty Years On*, while this track shared its title with a book by the German writer Hans Fallada. The song details Morrissey's perennial interest in minor celebrities and documents a period in the early Seventies when he lived and died in front of a television set. Speculative theories reckon the unnamed child star was Jack Wilde and the obscure ATV programme *Looks Familiar*. One of the album's stronger songs, it was recorded and completed early in the sessions.

## EVERYDAY IS LIKE SUNDAY

With a nuclear theme that recalled John Betjemen's 'Slough', this proved one of the highlights of the album and later emerged as a deserved Top 10 hit. Morrissey's satire on the English holiday resort is one of his best and, as he wittily observed, "The idea of a resort in Britain doesn't seem natural." The song came together surprisingly quickly with Stephen Street eagerly at the controls. "I hadn't heard the lyric before we went in the studio," he recalls. "I had the demo. We recorded it in exactly the same format as the demo. We might have changed the key to suit his voice. With Morrissey, two or three takes and you've got a vocal take. I know John Porter felt he didn't have it in that time, but with Morrissey I felt 'Catch him quick' because those early performances were superb." The classical flourish gave the song its haunting lilt – but don't be fooled into thinking that it's a string section you're hearing. It's just a trick.

## BENGALI IN PLATFORMS

"It's not being deliberately provocative," Morrissey insisted when confronted with the subject matter of what I would consider his most controversial and offensive song. It seems inconceivable that someone as supposedly well read as Morrissey could claim that this composition was not fraught with worrying ambiguities. Unlike his later so-called "racist" songs, which seemed naïvely criticised, this

deserves castigation for its infuriating condescension. The tone of the song is politely mocking, with Morrissey patronisingly commenting on his subject's rather displeasing sartorial style.

As if that's not enough, the singer takes on a role akin to that of a supercilious immigration officer, advising "it's hard enough when you belong here" (thereby implicitly suggesting that Bengalis do not belong here). Those satirically challenged listeners who defend Morrissey on the grounds that he is advising Bengalis of the difficulties of adjusting to western ways are clearly blind to the song's teasing condescension. Even the description of the Bengali is so outdated and stereotypical as to be laughable. I once defended Morrissey to myself by pointing out that the portrait of the Bengali was not set in the present but rather in the early Seventies, like several other songs on this album. This may yet be an over generous interpretation. The entire question of Morrissey's views on the Asian community past and present is a debate that still causes friction among his followers. Here the tone says as much as the lyrics and even the Indian sounding violin adds a slight air of ridicule to the proceedings.

## ANGEL, ANGEL, DOWN WE GO TOGETHER

This time the string section is in force for Morrissey's plea to a potential suicide. The Angel persona is so close to Morrissey's world view that he might almost be addressing himself in a mirror. "I'd demoed that with Morrissey at home," recalls Stephen Street, "so I knew the lyric... I wanted to do it with a proper string section, which I did". Certainly, the orchestration suits Morrissey's voice, adding a poignant edge to the lyrics.

## LATE NIGHT, MAUDLIN STREET

This seven and a half minute sentimental opus contained some of Morrissey's most self-pitying lyrics, alleviated by some of his most humorous. He sets the scene in 1972, amid a backdrop of power cuts and house moves, and an inner battle against ugliness, pill taking, family death and fantasy love. The arrangement plays up the pathos, but Morrissey cannot resist some moments of self-effacing comedy. The phrase "Goodbye house, goodbye stairs" sounds like Morrissey has been listening to Neil's version of 'Hole In My Shoe'. The bathos reaches an apogee with the classic and oft repeated line, "Me – without clothes? Well a nation turns its back and gags."

Vini Reilly's contribution to the song was particularly notable here. "The one I really liked was 'Maudlin Street'," he stresses, "simply because when we did it most of the chords were mine and my particular style of playing, even though the structure of the song was Stephen Street's". The producer, while crediting Reilly's excellent work, corrects his point about the chord sequence. "I did give Vini a lot of room," he points out. "But I can play you the demo of that and you can tell straight away that it's 'Late Night, Maudlin Street'. I needed Vini to put in one of those ambient guitar lines... The chords were the same, just a different key. Exactly the same chords. The one chord he changed was the first chord which he made a G Major 7th instead of a G Major. The rest of the chords were exactly the same as the demo, but a different key. Obviously, there's more than one way to play a chord – he might not have played them the way I would, but the main chords are there on the demo."

## SUEDEHEAD

Borrowed titles again – this time from Richard Allen's violent teen scream novel. Significantly, the lyrics had absolutely nothing to do with the book but reveal Morrissey's characteristic controlled vindictiveness. Missing from the lyric sheet is the closing line "It was a good lay" which raised some eyebrows among his following and provided more copy for the celibate expose hunters . Musically, the track was one of the most commercial Morrissey has ever recorded and provided his highest chart placing at number 5. This was the breakthrough song in the Morrissey/Street relationship. "I knew then it sounded really good and could work," Street told me. "But it wasn't until we got in a studio and cut a tune proper with Andrew and Vini, and Morrissey sung 'Suedehead' and I thought, 'Wow, this is great. It's going to work really well".

Vini Reilly stresses that Street deserves full credit for the song. " 'Suedehead' was more musically Stephen Street than any of the other things," he observes. "Yet that was the only thing people started to credit me with. In fact, the guitar break on 'Suedehead' is Stephen Street's tune. I play it but it's Stephen Street's

tune: the lead guitar, the chorus, the structure, the whole thing is Stephen Street. If he achieved one thing he did write a good single with Morrissey. It was a good choice and began very dramatically, very up and quite hard."

## BREAK UP THE FAMILY

A typical Morrissey lyric about the virtues of growing old while irresistibly looking at a painful past. As he explained: "The family in the song is the circle of friends where it almost seemed, because we were so identical, that for anybody to make any progress in life, we'd have to split up... And that's what happened." The subdued, simple arrangement complements the lyrics without ostentation. "I really like that song," Street notes. "I think it's a really nice vocal and very nice lyric. Great drumming from Andrew Paresi and some nice touches from Vini. Exactly the same format as I had on the demo, really. Again, I hadn't heard the lyric before we got into the studio".

## THE ORDINARY BOYS

Morrissey glorifies the elitism of the outsider, set against a waltz-time arrangement with additional orchestration. Stephen Street: "It's not one of my favourites. It was OK. I'd demoed that one with him so I knew exactly what it was. I'd heard the lyric before. It went down basically as we'd demoed it."

## I DON'T MIND
## IF YOU FORGET ME

Morrissey later complained that this album was severely weakened by several of the closing tracks and it's clear that this was one he had in mind. The lyrics are Morrissey by numbers: the old story of the maladjusted hero taking pyrrhic revenge on the person who once had the audacity to reject him. The arrangement is less than startling and the melody unmemorable. Even the normally effusive Street could not muster much enthusiasm for the track. "I don't think we ever captured that right on the album to be honest," he admits, "but it's a good scathing lyric... I did that guitar. I wanted it straight and quite simple so I knew I couldn't ask Vini to do it; he'd throw an incredible wobbly. It's not one of the stronger songs."

## DIAL A CLICHÉ

In keeping with the underlying theme of life in the early Seventies, Morrissey looks back at a dysfunctional youth when a fey image was still frowned upon. It's the old square peg in a round hole story which, as Morrissey knows, is something of a cliché. Hardly a candidate for Morrissey's Greatest Hits, it leads the album to an uneventful close. Stephen Street enjoyed the song, which was his attempt to write in a Beatlesque way. Guitarist Vini Reilly seemed less impressed and was clearly frustrated by his minimal creative role in the studio. "I put lots of hook lines in," he told me, "played French horn on a sampler on 'Dial A Cliché' and played fast and wild guitar on some tracks but, apart from that, there wasn't really anything satisfying for me. It was all too rigid, all too predictable."

## MARGARET ON A
## GUILLOTINE

In which Stephen Street's poignant melody is mischievously subverted by Morrissey into a vitriolic attack on the British Prime Minister. The lyrics pleading for the PM's death make even 'Meat Is Murder' sound subtle by comparison. The agitprop concludes with a macabre comic touch as we hear the decapitation followed by a deadly silence. This was a track that was often talked about but seldom loved.

It's interesting to note that 'Margaret On A Guillotine' was originally considered as the title to 'The Queen Is Dead'. However, you need only listen to those two songs to hear how much more fresher, inventive and accomplished The Smiths sounded when tackling political issues in song. It must have been a shock for Stephen Street when Morrissey presented his lyrics for this seemingly innocuous melody. "I was taken aback," the producer admits. "But, then again, it wasn't the first time I was taken aback. I felt it was a little bit strong. It was his domain. You don't mess with his lyrics. I remember thinking, it wasn't quite what I expected! He chuckled. He's got a dry sense of humour. I went, 'Phew!! Well, what can I say?' He'd just come upstairs from doing his vocals... All of that guitar is me apart from the acoustic at the end. I know people think Vini did all the guitar on that, but he didn't. I put down the rhythm guitar, Morrissey sang, Vini put on his little bit of Spanish guitar at the end which was beautiful and we put the guillotine chop from the BBC Sound Effects record. I think, in fact, it's a door being closed. It worked. It's not one of my favourites. I'm not going to defend it and say it's a brilliant piece of work, but it's an OK track."

# MORRISSEY
## "BONA DRAG"

# BONA DRAG

ORIGINAL/CURRENT ISSUE: HMV CDCSD 3788, OCTOBER 1990.

The history of 'Bona Drag' reveals Morrissey at another crucial crossroads in his career. Having completed 'Viva Hate' in surprisingly quick time, nobody could have anticipated the torturous delays and crisis of confidence that followed in its wake. At first it seemed that all was well and anticipation was high for a new album and possible tour. As early as December 1988 Morrissey had reunited with Rourke, Gannon and Joyce to play his first gig in two years at Wolverhampton Civic Hall. It was a chaotic affair which ended in pandemonium due to Morrissey's promise to offer free admission to followers who arrived wearing a Smiths T-shirt. In the event, over 17,000 fans converged on the city and the fraction that successfully gained admission witnessed Morrissey besieged by well wishers during an all too brief seven-minute set. If nothing else, it was proof positive that Morrissey could look forward to an invigorating tour whenever he chose to go back on the road.

With three other Smiths returning to camp, a full reunion seemed a distinct possibility, but it never came about. Marr was clearly not interested, while Gannon, Rourke and Joyce were in the strange position of performing with a singer whom they were also chasing to the High Court. What seemed the start of Morrissey's solo career became little more than an exercise in stasis.

The litigation dragged on, while Morrissey contented himself with releasing a series of singles, whose chart positions suggested that his charm was waning. A financial dispute with Stephen Street further complicated matters and persuaded Morrissey to find new collaborators. A tie-in with Clive Langer and Alan Winstanley began with 'Ouija Board, Ouija Board' which garnered the worst reviews of Morrissey's career and barely climbed into the Top 20. At least there was now the promise of a new album and by the end of 1989, Morrissey had several tracks ready. He announced that the new work would be called 'Bona Drag' but, as the weeks passed, it became clear that all was not well. The sessions ended abruptly with less than half an album completed and early the following year Morrissey announced that the project had been cancelled. Most of the completed tracks were issued as singles and the title 'Bona Drag' was retained for a compilation album that was issued to stop the gap between releases.

So, 18 months after 'Viva Hate', Morrissey had still not toured or completed a new album. Instead, we savoured a solo equivalent of 'Hatful Of Hollow', a pleasing enough release that once again showed how much fine work there was to be found on the flip sides of his 12-inch singles. It was a timely reminder, to Morrissey as much as his audience, that he had already recorded enough material to put together an album of excellent quality.

## PICCADILLY PALARE

Dogs howl as Morrissey plunges deep into his Madness fixation, complete with clanking piano and guest vocals from Suggs. This tale of male prostitution in the big city was an adventurous single and the last to reach the Top 20 before a long chart drought ensued. The Langer/ Winstanley influence is prominent and it's pleas-

ing to see Morrissey moving away from self-reflection to create new characters in song. His use of rent boy slang betrayed a grounding in *Round The Horne* and encouraged a spate of articles translating his "palare".

## INTERESTING DRUG

Another example of Morrissey as social commentator, this time condemning government youth schemes and championing the escapism of recreational drugs. In the wake of this composition, it was interesting to hear Morrissey admit that he had taken Ecstasy. Kirsty MacColl provides back-up vocals for what became Morrissey's fourth consecutive Top 10 hit. Incidentally, the lyric sheet claims there are "bad people on the rise", while Morrissey appears to sing "on the right". The video for the song saw right emphatically scratched on a blackboard as if to emphasise the correct interpretation.

## NOVEMBER SPAWNED A MONSTER

This powerful single was something of a return to form for Morrissey following the flack he received over 'Ouija Board, Ouija Board'. In common with 'Interesting Drug' and 'Piccadilly Palare' the lyrics are controversial, as Morrissey tackles the plight of the disabled. As ever with Morrissey, the tone and sentiments are riddled with ambiguity. What seems a genuine display of sympathy is subverted by the very power of the language, with phrases such as "twisted child" and "monster" presenting the invalid as seen by society. Yet the singer's own tone seems mocking at times and there is even a touch of sexual black comedy in the line about kissing the invalid "on the mouth or anywhere". Mary Margaret O'Hara's theatrical vocal outpouring is at once horrific, humane and comic – in keeping with Morrissey's ambiguous approach. The backing adds to the drama with some effective touches such as the harmonica break during O'Hara's babbling. Morrissey chooses to end the song on a note of pathetic fulfilment with the girl defiantly promising to purchase her own clothes.

## WILL NEVER MARRY

This is an edited version of one of those understated compositions which occasionally served as postscripts to Morrissey's singles. With its acceptance of the unremitting inevitability of loneliness, the song leaves no room for the usual disarming humour or ambiguity.

## SUCH A LITTLE THING MAKES SUCH A BIG DIFFERENCE

The flip side of 'Interesting Drug', this was among the slightest of songs in the Morrissey canon. Its dull arrangement is rescued only by a drop of Morrissey petulance when he complains about people that "keep their brains between their legs". Surprisingly, the song was used in concert and worked well live.

## THE LAST OF THE FAMOUS INTERNATIONAL PLAYBOYS

Morrissey's abiding affection for criminal glamour reached its apogee with this confused tale of a lad entranced by the Krays. Morrissey attempted to dissociate himself from the character in the song when he told the NME: "I don't have admiration for the Kray Twins at all but am fascinated and almost amused that they've been confused with minor celebrities. In their day they were, but they murdered. I think the attention they received and continue to receive elevates them to the state of minor celebrities." When asked the identity of the unnamed international playboys, however, he added an autobiographical touch by suggesting that they were Devoto, Bolan, Bowie and himself. One of the more amusing aspects of this song was that it actually prompted a discerning reply from the still imprisoned Reggie Kray who opined, "I liked the tune but I thought the lyrics in their entirety were lacking a little."

## OUIJA BOARD, OUIJA BOARD

This single provided the first serious backlash of Morrissey's solo career. It was lambasted in the press and failed to emulate the Top 10 success of its predecessors. Yet, it was an amusing enough song and not as uncommercial as critical opinion dictated. As usual, Morrissey cannot resist turning the wit upon himself as he relates the perils of after life communication. From beyond the grave, his reluctant old friend dismisses his advances with the surly riposte, "Steven – Push Off!"

## HAIRDRESSER ON FIRE

Without doubt, this was one of Morrissey's most attractive and witty songs and its inclusion on the album was an absolute delight. Its wonderfully bathetic, with Morrissey lightly

satirising the hairdresser as psychic healer. The backing, including a mock dramatic orchestral opening, xylophone chimes and some spectacular Vini Reilly guitar work, adds to the exuberant air. Morrissey tops it off with his engaging vocal mannerisms and the result is possibly the best B-side of his solo career.

## EVERYDAY IS LIKE SUNDAY

It seems strange to hear this famous song so late into the album. Perhaps its placing was indicative of Morrissey's ambiguous feelings about featuring so recent an album track on successive releases.

## HE KNOWS I'D LOVE TO SEE HIM

The fact that Morrissey hadn't seen Johnny Marr since the Smiths' split was enough to convince the world that this was a thinly disguised letter to the guitarist. Maybe it was; then again, it could have been directed towards Johnny Daly, and who knows who else. Midway through the song Morrissey switches attention to a recent drama in his life when he was interviewed by the police after his comments on Margaret Thatcher. After listening to the constabulary's caustic comments on his bedroom radicalism and lazy ways, he could only agree with them. The tone of languid resignation in the words "I know I do" sums up his world view with a wonderful flourish of irony.

## YES, I AM BLIND

Co-written by Andy Rourke, this was far from the bassist's best work with Morrissey and you can't help feeling that 'Girl Least Likely To' would have been a better choice. Morrissey invokes a Marlovian atheism recalling Tamburlaine's cry for God to come down from the heavens. The anti-Christian sentiments in the last verse are undeveloped, just at the point when they are getting interesting.

## LUCKY LISP

The title puns on Cliff Richard's 'Lucky Lips' as Morrissey humorously indulges his hero worship with some light ironic touches. So whom did Morrissey have in mind? Again, the name Johnny Marr comes to mind, especially when you consider how he pronounces his "r" and "w" sounds.

## SUEDEHEAD

The most successful song of Morrissey's solo career is tucked away almost unnoticed as the penultimate track on the album. For those who bought 'Viva Hate' this was one single too many and Morrissey was probably aware of this. Its inclusion finally draws attention to those other tracks that failed to win a place on the compilation: 'I Know Very Well How I Got My Name', 'Oh Well, I'll Never Learn', 'Sister I'm A Poet', 'Michael's Bones', 'East West', 'Girl Least Likely To', 'Get Off The Stage' and 'At Amber'. At least there is ample opportunity now for a sequel to take in these non-album titles... but beware the later 'The World Of Morrissey'.

## DISAPPOINTED

This had to be the closing track, given its marvellously humorous ending. As Morrissey announces that this may be the last song he will ever sing, the assembled crew cheer, then jeer when he adds that he's again changed his mind. The "Goodnight and thank you" not only concludes the album on an appropriate note, but serves as a farewell to Vini Reilly whose simmering guitar work, alongside Paresi's powerful drumming, makes this track one of the most memorable of Morrissey's minor works.

# KILL UNCLE

ORIGINAL/CURRENT ISSUE: HMV CDCSD 3789, MARCH 1991.

**Five months after 'Bona Drag', the true follow-up to 'Viva Hate' finally appeared. This was the end of Morrissey's dark period of indecision as the album was soon followed by his first full UK tour as a solo performer. Extensive tours of the USA and Japan came next as Morrissey confirmed that he had finally found a group with whom he felt comfortable playing on stage. In the midst of all this, of course, was that strange and paltry album 'Kill Uncle'.**

Looking back to 1991 the reviews are salutary. *Melody Maker*'s Steve Sutherland savaged the album and left readers in no doubt that he considered the singer a sorry, spent force. Other reviewers were more charitable, even enthusiastic. The *NME* reckoned the album was worth an exceptionally generous 8 out of 10, while the equally youth-oriented *Select* proffered an impressive 4 out of 5 rating. The chart statistics gave a truer reflection of the album's worth. Despite the long delays and anticipation the LP only entered at number 8 and plummeted soon after. It is not too difficult to see why. At just over 33 minutes in length, it was insubstantial in quantity and equally disappointing in quality. Although Langer and Winstanley were highly accomplished producers with a formidable track

record, their relationship with Morrissey seemed ill-starred. The same criticisms could be levelled against the singer's new writing collaborator Mark E. Nevin whose contributions seemed at best erratic, at worst uninspired. In fairness, he was severely handicapped by Morrissey's demands for tapes to be sent through the post without prior consultation or extensive feedback. Deciding upon suitable material seemed largely pot luck. While some tracks were mildly impressive, too many others were dull as dish water, with poor melodies and some of the worst lyrics of Morrissey's career.

The timing of the world tour proved crucial for it distracted from the more negative aspects of the album and gave critics the opportunity to focus on Morrissey's strengths as a performer. In concert, the weaker moments of 'Kill Uncle' were either disguised or improved and the album ultimately served as a token memento of Morrissey's return to centre stage. When the tour ended, however, the niggling questions returned. Was Morrissey effectively a jaded creative force now reduced to parodying his finer moments in the Smiths? Was 'Kill Uncle' the nadir of his career, or could there be even worse to follow?

## OUR FRANK

The twin influences of Madness and Roxy Music are evident on this single which, despite being issued prior to the album's release, only climbed as high as number 26. Morrissey's plea for some frivolous conversation is set against a raga-like violin backing. Some of the vocal effects come courtesy of an Eventide Harmoniser. The original demo of this recording was more stark than one might have expected. "It was quite folky when we started," noted Clive Langer. "I think we booted it up a bit".

## ASIAN RUT

Classically trained violinist Nawazish Ali Khan added further raga touches to this track which complemented the theme of racial unrest.

Morrissey's melodrama focuses on the righteous vengeance of an Asian boy who is felled in an uneven fight against white oppressors. Unlike 'Bengali In Platforms' the lyrics do not invite condemnation, although Morrissey still suffered criticism in some quarters simply for tackling the racial theme. Musically, the harmonium is noticeable on the track. "It was a bit out of tune so we had to varispeed the tape," explained Alan Winstanley.

## SING YOUR LIFE

Morrissey's love of simple pop is summed up in this track. The minimal chord sequence and delicate arrangement enhance his DIY guide to pop stardom. Issued as a single, the song reached a paltry number 33, ending Morrissey's run of Top 30 hits. Its slight air was clearly of concern to the producers, who brought in keyboard player Steve Heart to add some colour to the arrangement. As Clive Langer told journalist Tom Doyle: "We gave Morrissey's voice that early Sixties' vocal sound with the short delay. I think the song just gets better and better as it goes along, which is good because it's so frighteningly lightweight. Hopefully, it's a charming song which displays a nice sense of humour".

## MUTE WITNESS

Co-written by Clive Langer, this tune owed much to the influence of Roxy Music. Indeed, the opening sounds uncannily like 'Virginia Plain'. Lyrically, Morrissey attempts a comedy of the afflicted, just as he had done in parts of 'November Spawned A Monster'. Here, the tone is lightly mocking and the words laced with benign condescension as the narrator ushers the "hopeless" witness into a taxi with the dismissively polite "my dear" conclusion.

Although it's refreshing to see Morrissey moving away from self-analysis, it has to be said that the subject matter here is neither riveting nor particularly funny. At least, the singing is confident, and Langer, like Street and Reilly before him, noted the tendency to place vocals in unexpected parts of the song. "Morrissey's backing vocal in the instrumental is quite amazing," he enthused. "In fact, he didn't put it in the instrumental, he put it in the chorus, but then we moved it. But he's got a great sort of pop sense which people don't realise. I think for a long time he was singing within a certain range and I think he's opened up a little now."

## KING LEER

This appallingly bad pun was made worse by the lyrics, which were probably the worst of Morrissey's career, thus far. The melody and arrangement were little better and the entire thing testifies to a lack of inspiration. Even Clive Langer admitted that it was at best "a bit ordinary".

## FOUND FOUND FOUND

According to Langer this tune was "knocked out in about five minutes". Although an obvious attempt to add some weight to the proceedings it at least distracted attention from the lighter material on the album. Mark Nevin plays a Hofner Violin bass, just like Paul McCartney, while Langer provides the heavy guitar work. The lyrics are platitudinous and sound as rushed as the music. Interestingly, it's been stated in numerous magazines that the subject of the song is R.E.M.'s Michael Stipe, although the conjecture lacks foundation. During an interview with *Select,* Morrissey discussed this song and then in the very next question was asked about his recent friendship with Stipe. Neither he nor the journalist made any connections between the song and Stipe but the placing of the quotes encouraged others in search of good copy to connect the two.

## DRIVING YOUR GIRLFRIEND HOME

Morrissey plays father confessor in another of those mini-dramas in which he has always excelled. The appearance of Linder on backing vocals is endearing and the song might have been even better if she had been allowed to sing the girlfriend's part. This was probably the most attractive song on the album but a little too fragile to release as a single.

## THE HARSH TRUTH OF THE CAMERA EYE

Dull lyrics and a turgid arrangement ultimately cripple this song which nevertheless drags on for over five minutes. As Langer explained: "We recorded this track with a long ending, and when Steve Heart came in to do the keyboards, the piano and sound effects, he just kept going on to the end. The album needed a bit of playing, a bit of something loose. Also, it doesn't sound like anyone else." The sampled sounds seem designed to add some life to the track,

but do not prove sufficiently diverting. On reflection, the song's sole saving grace is the psychologically revealing last verse wherein Morrissey sums up his narcissistic insecurity in the words: "I would just sooner be blindly loved".

## (I'M) THE END OF THE FAMILY LINE

More self-mythologising from Morrissey in this slight but vaguely interesting speculation on his decaying dynasty. Like so many songs on this album, the composition seems fragmentary and undeveloped. Those who take Morrissey's words literally may be disappointed to learn that he is not the last of the Morrissey family line. In fact it was this song that prompted me to commission Pete Frame to draw a family tree revealing the still flourishing Morrissey clan.

## THERE'S A PLACE IN HELL FOR ME AND MY FRIENDS

The funereal piano and familiarly maudlin tone close the album on a suitably anti-climactic note as Morrissey speculates on the redeeming aspects of damnation. Having ended his mortal life on the previous track, he pictures himself among his friends in hell. The arrangement is deliberately minimalist with the Mark Nevin piano work being lifted from a cassette rather than recorded in the studio. All in all, it proved an unusual closing track to Morrissey's strangest and most disappointing album.

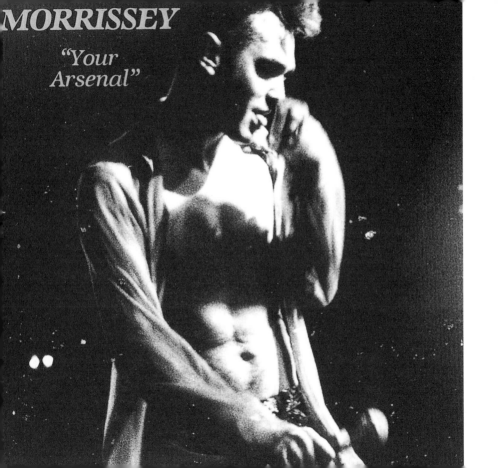

# MORRISSEY

## "Your Arsenal"

# YOUR ARSENAL

ORIGINAL/CURRENT ISSUE: HMV CDCSD 3790, JULY 1992.

**M**orrissey took to the road for a world tour after 'Kill Uncle' and it was during this period that his rockabilly style backing group emerged as a formidable unit. During the US leg of the tour, the singer was joined on-stage by David Bowie for a rendition of 'Cosmic Dancer'. Some months later, Morrissey would recruit Bowie's former guitarist as his latest producer.

The choice turned out to be an inspired one. The resulting album was, in almost every respect, the complete opposite of its predecessor. Instead of low key arrangements and lightweight, reflective tunes, Morrissey seemed hell bent on reclaiming the oompah glam rock sound of his teenage years. With Mark Nevin only available for a couple of songs, the singer turned to guitarist Alain Whyte who wrote the majority of the album. What emerged was a genuine group sound; the obvious legacy of months spent on the road. It did not escape the public's attention that Morrissey had at last found a group of musicians with whom he could interact as if in a gang. Significantly, 'Your Arsenal' did not include a lyric sheet, a sure sign that Morrissey wanted to shift attention away from himself and encourage a more direct appreciation of the music rather than the authorial sentiments.

It was also interesting to note that neither of his last two singles, 'My Love Life' and 'Pregnant For The Last Time' were deemed necessary to pad out the album. Here was a work which demanded all new material. At a time when Morrissey's career seemed in the descendent, the album was the ultimate confidence booster. Critical reaction was almost universally favourable and its chart placing at number 4 in the UK was a significant improvement on 'Kill Uncle'. Equally importantly, 'Your Arsenal' gave Morrissey his first real taste of success in the US charts and suggested that he could now go on to establish himself as a world-wide star, if he chose.

## YOU'RE GONNA NEED SOMEONE ON YOUR SIDE

The opening riff of the album neatly fuses Eddie Cochran's 'Something Else' with 'The Batman Theme' to create an arresting backdrop in marked contrast to the insipid sound of 'Kill Uncle'. For the first time in ages, Morrissey actually sounds as if he's part of a group again. Lyrically, the song stresses the need for friends, a theme that would be developed more fully on his next studio album.

## GLAMOROUS GLUE

Mick Ronson's influence is strikingly evident here as Morrissey indulges himself in a veritable cornucopia of glam rock. Half of the fun lies in spotting the influences which take in Bowie, The Sweet's 'Blockbuster' and Gary Glitter's 'Rock And Roll (Parts 1 and 2)'. Lyrically, the song reiterates Morrissey's love/hate relationship with the USA and his regrets about England's lost glories. The much quoted line "We look to Los Angeles for the language we use: London is dead" summed up his feelings of disillusionment. As he explained: "What I mean by this is all television and radio broadcasters now speak with American accents.

The English news is very interesting because now it's totally focused on America. Everything that happens in America is constantly reported on the English news while in America England is never referred to and British politics are completely meaningless. I mean the country could completely explode and disappear into outer space and America would not mention that on the daily news".

## WE'LL LET YOU KNOW

Warming to this theme, Morrissey adopts the persona of an English football hooligan as a dubious embodiment of enduring patriotism. In discussing the song, Morrissey explained his feelings about soccer thugs to Q magazine : "I understand the level of patriotism, the level of frustration and the level of jubilance. I understand the overall character. I understand their aggression and I understand why it must be released... When I see reports on the television about hooliganism in Sweden and Denmark or somewhere I'm actually amused... As long as people don't die, I am amused." Interestingly, the song ends with the sounds of battle.

## THE NATIONAL FRONT DISCO

The nationalist theme continues on this ominously titled and soon to be controversial lyric. Inevitably, the song attracted anti-racist diatribes in certain sections of the press and particular attention was paid to the inflammatory line "England For The English". Few pointed out that it was actually far less offensive and ambiguous than 'Bengali In Platforms'. In adopting the persona of Davey, Morrissey paints a vivid picture of an ordinary, suburban boy "lost" to the lure of the NF. The references to the love of a country that doesn't exist pinpoints the follies of right wing nationalism rather than promoting its philosophies. Finally, the idea of a National Front Disco is such a ludicrous proposition that it adds a satirical punch to the entire issue. The fact that the song, unlike 'Bengali In Platforms' or 'Asian Rut', is such a commercial, catchy song merely adds to its lack of serious intent.

## CERTAIN PEOPLE I KNOW

This song testifies to Morrissey's enduring love of Marc Bolan with a hook line that recalls 'Ride A White Swan'. A limited edition version of the track was later issued featuring a pastiche sleeve with Morrissey in Bolan pose pictured underneath the word "Moz" instead of "T Rex". As the third single issued from the album, its chart placing was always likely to be low and a peak of number 35 proved worse than even 'Sing Your Life'.

## WE HATE IT WHEN OUR FRIENDS BECOME SUCCESSFUL

Issued as a single three months before the album's release, this light effort returned Morrissey to the Top 20. The clever title belied the banal lyrics, but at least the tune was hummable, short and bitter. The back stabbing locals that Morrissey satirises seem not a million miles away from the cynical, embittered person he would have been if pop star fame had proved elusive. As Morrissey explained to Adrian Deevoy: "There's the most vicious sense of competition in Manchester... So many jealous, vile creatures. This is what the song 'We Hate It When Our Friends Become Successful' is about. In Manchester, you are accepted as long as you are scrambling and on your knees. But if you have any success or are independent or a free spirit, they hate your guts."

## YOU'RE THE ONE FOR ME, FATTY

Having previously championed the physically and mentally handicapped, the deformed and the culturally alienated, it's good to see Morrissey inverting love song tradition by cooing the overweight. It may be worth noting that as an adolescent Steven had no time for fatties and was wont to blame them for eating too much. Another Top 20 reward for catchy banality, the song was at least memorable as a comic romp. In situating the action in Battersea, Morrissey recalled Nell Dunn's *Up The Junction*. Fans were left with a parlour guessing game of identifying the "fatty" of the title, resulting in such humorous nominations as Oscar Wilde, Kirsty MacColl, post-Smiths Johnny Marr and even Morrissey himself, whose girth had grown noticeably during this period.

## SEASICK, YET STILL DOCKED

For older Morrissey fans, this was undoubtedly the album's crowning achievement. A work of bitter poignancy, the song seemed to embrace all of Morrissey's neuroses. There's the despair of never being able to find love ("There is no way"), earnest self deprecation ("I've got no charm"), self pity ("No one has ever given me anything") and romantic narcissism ("My love is as sharp as a needle in your eye/You'd be such a fool to pass it by"). The overall effect is strangely alluring and the enticing arrangement provides an almost Smiths-like quality to the track. It seems both impressive and disconcerting to observe the ease with which the 33-year-old singer draws on experiences more appropriate to a tortured adolescent, but such is the nature of Morrissey's appeal.

## I KNOW IT'S GONNA HAPPEN SOMEDAY

In which Morrissey reinvents himself as an early Fifties balladeer. This is the closest he has ever come to re-creating the sound and ambience of those early pre-Beatles singles that he so loved. The lilt is attractive conjuring up images of Johnnie Ray and other lost icons. Hammy radio effects actually work well here. The final accolade for Morrissey came with David Bowie's decision to record a cover version of the song. At last, Morrissey's teenage hero was eating from his hand.

## TOMORROW

With a title borrowed from Sandie Shaw's 1966 Top 10 hit, Morrissey poses the reluctant question "Does it have to come?" It's an intriguing coda in which many of his old themes collide: furtive sexuality, psychosomatic illness and frustration. There's even a cry to arms in the arch message to those already sharpening their critical knives in anticipation of a killing: "You don't think I'll make it – I never said I wanted to, did I?" A fascinating conclusion to an album that was a welcome return to form.

# BEETHOVEN WAS DEAF

ORIGINAL/CURRENT ISSUE: PARLOPHONE CDCSD 3791, MAY 1993.

Following 'Your Arsenal', Morrissey could afford to feel optimistic about the response to his live performances and this was confirmed when he sold out the Hollywood Bowl in record time. Back in England, however, all was far from well. Branching out from his usual fan base, the singer had agreed to appear on the same bill as Madness for two evenings at Finsbury Park. It was to prove a costly error. The Madstock affair ended in disarray and controversy when Morrissey appeared on-stage clad in a Union Jack flag. The Nutty Boys' hard core followers took exception and pilloried the singer with a variety of missiles. After a relatively short set, he left the stage and refused to fulfil his engagement the following evening.

Meanwhile, the *NME* reopened the perennial "Is Morrissey A Racist?" debate which prompted a barrage of letters, defending and condemning the singer for his ambiguous use of right wing imagery. The furore continued and cast a shadow over the tour, with Morrissey infrequently castigating the music paper on-stage. It was a strange time for Morrissey who otherwise appeared to be at his most popular. He had been performing Suede's 'My Insatiable One' in concert, thereby indicating that he was still in touch with the indie scene; Bowie had covered 'I Know It's Gonna Happen Someday'; and even the unlikely figure of Kevin Rowland had come to his defence in the music press.

Throughout this time, his concerts were as frenzied as ever, with energetic fans clambering on-stage at every opportunity. The singer's upswing in commercial favour persuaded him to sanction the release of a live album, which came as something of a surprise. The Smiths had never issued a live recording in their lifetime, but after three studio albums and a compilation, Morrissey and EMI felt that the time was right for the bard to satiate the need. Although the live work contained three songs previously unavailable on album, it was in most respects a predictable tour memento. Nine of the ten songs featured on 'Your Arsenal' reappeared, which seemed a high ratio in the circumstances. At least Morrissey came close to capturing a complete concert on record, although three songs escaped: 'Tomorrow', 'Alsatian Cousin' and 'The Last Of The International Playboys'. To confuse matters, there was a bit of jiggery pokery in the ordering and selection of tracks. According to the accompanying notes, the album was taped at the Zenith in Paris on 22 December 1992. However, two tracks, 'The National Front Disco' and 'He Knows I'd Love To See Him', were culled from the London Astoria show two days before. Such minor inconsistencies aside, the album was a faithful representation of Morrissey's live shows of the period, and the remixing by Bob Clearmountain did not rob the set of its inchoate charm.

## YOU'RE THE ONE FOR ME, FATTY

The Paris set is immediately resequenced so that this bouncy single opens proceedings rather than 'We Hate It When Our Friends Become Successful'. Here, the group is given a freer hand and the ode to 'Fatty' sounds more raucous and exuberant than its studio counterpart.

## CERTAIN PEOPLE I KNOW

Another former single follows, maintaining the commercial opening to the album. The group are again in noticeably good form, fusing Bolan-style riffs with a distinct rockabilly edge. The slightly cod ending seems quite appealing too.

## THE NATIONAL FRONT DISCO

In concert, it's rather disconcerting to hear the extent to which this song seems to function as a clarion call as Morrissey sings the words "England For The English". The satirical subtleties are sacrificed before the singalong chorus which the audience is happy to ape. Morrissey had already admitted his own views on racial disharmony in an interview with $Q$ magazine prior to the album's release. In view of his Paris performance, it is interesting to observe that he was equally pessimistic about Anglo-French relations. "I don't really think black and white people will ever really get on or like each other," he stressed. "I don't really think they ever will. The French will never like the English. The English will never like the French. That tunnel will collapse."

Musically, the live version of 'The National Front Disco' has a much harder edge, with a dramatic conclusion during which the group fly across the stage like exploding rockets colliding in a frenzy of guitar feedback. Amid the cacophony a few notes of Jimi Hendrix's 'Purple Haze' escape from the ether.

## NOVEMBER SPAWNED A MONSTER

The audience is teased by the opening of 'Ouija Board, Ouija Board' before Morrissey abruptly bursts into 'November Spawned A Monster'. He provides a suitably dramatic reading of the song, with the group adding a solid, tight backing. The crowd's enthusiasm and curiosity is evident as the song approaches the section where Mary Margaret O'Hara appears on the studio version. She is replaced by some handclaps and fierce drumming as Morrissey takes the song to an eventful close. The most revealing part of the song occurs when Morrissey almost bursts into laughter while singing "Oh, no, no, no", thereby indicating the underlying comic revulsion in the lyrics.

## SEASICK, YET STILL DOCKED

The crowd enthusiastically chant Morrissey's

name as a preamble to the most affecting song from 'Your Arsenal'. This is not as powerful as the excellent album version but sounds reasonable enough in a live context. Perhaps a more imaginative arrangement would have been better.

## THE LOOP

Something of a rarity, this non-album song was previously available on the 12-inch version of 'Sing Your Life'. The live version is adequate but remains something of a filler. It seems clear why Morrissey chose to leave the tune off an album, for it is not one of his more memorable compositions. However, it does give the group a chance to show off their love of late Fifties' instrumentals.

## SISTER I'M A POET

Another non-album song, this first appeared on the 12-inch version of 'Everyday Is Like Sunday' and also featured in the video *Hulmerist*. The Paris version is not the best reading of the song, but you still come away wondering what Morrissey is referring to in those oblique lyrics in which the word "poet" is conspicuous by its absence. Over the years this song has become a live favourite, which partly compensates for its surprising failure to appear on 'Bona Drag'.

## JACK THE RIPPER

The trilogy of non-album songs is completed with this, the flip side of 'Certain People I Know'. At one point this live version was considered as a possible single, but the idea was vetoed. However, it was issued as a DJ-only promotional release. It's certainly one of Morrissey's better B-sides and the ghost train guitar sound provides an effectively eerie backing. On reflection, Morrissey was fortunate to escape further controversy with this title. When Screaming Lord Sutch performed his song of the same title not so long ago, his concerts were boycotted by feminist protesters.

## SUCH A LITTLE THING MAKES SUCH A BIG DIFFERENCE

Morrissey's vocal wavers noticeably on this live version, but the effect is pleasing. Indeed, the song works surprisingly well in Paris, with the power chords adding a beefier backing to the more restrained original.

## I KNOW IT'S GONNA HAPPEN SOMEDAY

There is no time for a break as 'Such A Little Thing Makes Such A Big Difference' segues seamlessly into this big ballad. Morrissey provides a sustained performance throughout and the arrangement is inventive with an engagingly chaotic backing.

## WE'LL LET YOU KNOW

There seems little to say about this live version which is remarkably faithful to its studio counterpart. Indeed, such over-familiarity weakens the power of several of these songs. At least, the mixing is impressive and the vocals seem particularly well recorded.

## SUEDEHEAD

Morrissey's first single is an obvious crowd favourite and is greeted by loud cheers. When the group first played this song live it was very ragged, but over the years they have improved their reading. Morrissey enjoys some playful vocal gulping and even includes some extra lyrics. The coda, with the reference to "a good lay" is sung loud and clear without ambiguity. Loud applause follows.

## HE KNOWS I'D LOVE TO SEE HIM

This song was slotted in from the London Astoria gig two days before and abruptly changes the mood of the set. It is to the group's credit that this sounds more forceful than the languid studio version and works far better in concert than might have been anticipated.

## YOU'RE GONNA NEED SOMEONE ON YOUR SIDE

Neatly placed on the album, this fierce upbeat rocker allows the group full rein to show their credentials, which they do with considerable aplomb.

## GLAMOROUS GLUE

The uptempo feel continues on this, the most bombastic track on the album. The group is allowed to improvise somewhat and finally go wild as the song reaches a powerful conclusion, amid a burst of interweaving guitars and feedback.

## WE HATE IT WHEN OUR FRIENDS BECOME SUCCESSFUL

A pure singalong in which the French audience follow every nuance of Morrissey's vocal. This is more passionate and energetic than the anodyne single and, taken at a faster pace, provides an exciting and pleasant ending to the album. Ironically, this actually opened the show in Paris, but you'd never guess that listening to the emphatic close. Tagged on to the end is a brief "Thank you, I love you. Goodbye" and the show is over.

# MORRISSEY

## "VAUXHALL AND I"

# VAUXHALL AND I

ORIGINAL/CURRENT ISSUE PARLOPHONE CDPCSD 148

**A**fter all the hullabaloo over 'Your Arsenal' and Morrissey's impressive invasion of America, 1993 looked likely to be a year of consolidation. In the background, however, further dramatic events were taking place which caused Morrissey to ponder on friendships past and present.

In the fallout of *The Severed Alliance*, Andy Rourke returned as an embittered litigant to take his place behind Mike Joyce who was still in the process of chasing Morrissey through the High Court over the question of Smiths monies. Meanwhile, Rough Trade ceased trading and the entire Smiths catalogue reverted to Morrissey and Marr, only to be sold on to Warner Brothers. News gradually reached the press that Morrissey and Marr were not only back in contact but had successfully resolved their former differences and were now fast friends. Inevitably, there was speculation about a possible Smiths reunion, with Marr adding the proviso that if ever such a thing happened it would more likely be a Morrissey/Marr collaboration. Andy Rourke was also keenly aware of the dangers of attempting to turn back the clock. "If we all did

agree to get back together, it'd probably be a bad move," he told me. "It could be a real letdown. We've all changed. We've all moved on. Musically, we couldn't really sound like that anymore. Maybe we could, you never know until you've tried it. But in the press it would always look like a money-making thing . Like that's the whole reason we'd reform – to do a massive tour, a reunion album, make a lot of money and split up again."

With the substantial profit Morrissey had made from selling his back catalogue and the current standing of his career internationally, it was clear that he certainly did not need the money. Moreover, his negative comments about Rourke and Joyce in the music press suggested that his fondness for them had long since past. If old friends were at a premium then some of the newer ones seemed in danger of extinction. In the space of a few short months Tim Broad, Nigel Thomas and Mick Ronson all passed away. The singer had lost his video director, manger and producer at a point when he might otherwise have been celebrating a major career breakthrough.

Those losses had a profound effect on Morrissey and permeated the writing and recording of his next album. It was undoubtedly his most subdued record to date, but arguably his finest as a soloist. Gone were the trite lyrics that had blighted 'Kill Uncle' and parts of 'Your Arsenal'. Instead, Morrissey hit top form with some of the finest writing of his career. The album was rightly hailed as a major work with five star reviews dominating magazine listings. Steve Lillywhite's production, which might have been too smooth for many fans' tastes, perfectly extracted the melancholic tinge from the songs while adding a musical thrust which was appealing and effective. What proved most impressive was Morrissey's new found consistency and ability to fashion two contrasting but exceptional studio albums in succession. Originally, 'Vauxhall And I' was scheduled for release as early as November 1993, but was delayed by several months, a fate that also

befell 'Interlude' the singer's collaboration with Siouxsie Sioux.

## NOW MY HEART IS FULL

Distorted guitars open the album as Morrissey launches into the ominous line, "There's gonna be some trouble". What emerges is both a serious and celebratory acknowledgement of the onset of happiness, an emotion which Morrissey, for once cannot express in words ("I just can't explain"). Not for the first time, Morrissey finds solace in the gang mentality, this time namedropping the deviant characters in Graham Greene's *Brighton Rock*, a novel that was adapted for film, with Richard Attenborough playing the part of the psychopath Pinkie.

## SPRING-HEELED JIM

Morrissey's ambivalent hero worship of glamorous wide boys and flash Harrys continues with this tale of young hedonism, womanising and live-for-today recklessness. By the close, however, the character feels the chill of passing time and encroaching age. In order to add to the atmosphere, there is a sample from the Fifties' television documentary, *We Are The Lambeth Boys*.

## BILLY BUDD

This is the key gay song on the album, the title borrowed from Herman Melville's famous short story of incorruptible innocence faced with inexplicable evil. It seems more likely that Morrissey took his inspiration from the film version, which starred his old idol Terence Stamp. The delay in the album's release ensured that the lines "It's 12 years on... and I took up with you" took on a particular resonance. For it was now 12 years since Morrissey had first teamed up with Marr and it was well known that they had recently reconciled their old differences. The fact that the aforementioned lines are followed by what sounds like a light pastiche of Marr's pyrotechnic work on 'The Queen Is Dead' merely adds to the song's mysterious charm.

## HOLD ON TO YOUR FRIENDS

Feelings of vulnerability and persecution are dominant themes on this album, and this is a key track in that mode. "It was written about somebody I know in relation to their treatment towards me," Morrissey explained. "I'm simply waiting for people to do something damaging and they inevitably do." The motto appears to be that with enemies so prolific, why squander time turning on friends. There is also criticism of a certain fair weather friend who only calls the bard when depressed and ignores him in happier times. Who can he be referring to?

## THE MORE YOU IGNORE ME, THE CLOSER I GET

As a single, this was something of a return to form, both lyrically and melodically, and gave Morrissey his first Top 10 hit since 'Interesting Drug' five years before. His presentation of love as a chess game, complete with connotations of vengeance if unrequited contains some impressive lines with analogies to high court judges and even some appropriately fiscal imagery. Steve Lillywhite's upfront production greatly enhances the song while Boz Boorer adds a solid, radio friendly riff.

## WHY DON'T YOU FIND OUT FOR YOURSELF

Morrissey's mini-thesis on the plight of the pop star is far more impressive than his previous excursion in such territory, 'Paint A Vulgar Picture'. Here, he rails against money-grubbers, manipulators, skin peelers, backstabbers and those that dare to write disparagingly about his career ("Don't rake up my mistakes/I know exactly what they are'). I wonder who he had in mind! There is, at least, stoical acceptance and an almost painful shrug of the shoulders in the closing rejoinder, "That's just the way it goes."

## I AM HATED FOR LOVING

A delicate arrangement frames another bout of paranoia, this time aimed at anonymous callers and poison pen pushers. The echo on Morrissey's voice adds a poignant element to an otherwise average composition. Although the songs begin to overstate the central theme here, the sheer air of defiance that Morrissey oozes proves compelling.

## LIFEGUARD SLEEPING, GIRL DROWNING

There's a sprinkling of the old Morrissey misogyny in this tale of an attention seeking woman who tries his patience once too often. A string quartet is present here, alongside an impressive clarinet arrangement from Boz Boorer. Morrissey's whispered, sensual vocal

is extremely seductive and the composition emerges as one of his most unusual and intriguing to date.

## USED TO BE A SWEET BOY

At a crucial stage in the album, Morrissey addresses the very root of his childhood neuroses. Here, for the first time on record, he expresses his uneasy and still unresolved relationship with his father. The song followed recent comments from the singer about the break up of his parents' marriage when he was 17. The backing, with piano and compressed harmonies, is incredibly evocative and makes this the most moving composition on the album.

## THE LAZY SUNBATHERS

This could be interpreted as a satire of both Hollywood and Costa Rica values, as sun worshippers are portrayed as immune even to the news of a probable nuclear war. The sound effects include what appears to be nuclear rain in the background, or perhaps just splashing waves. The theme is very similar to that evoked in 'Everyday Is Like Sunday' in which seaside escapades and nuclear war were uneasily joined.

## SPEEDWAY

More playfulness from Morrissey in which he keeps his critics guessing again by suggesting that the rumours that kept him grounded were not entirely unfounded. The *NME* interpreted this as an admission that there was some truth in the racist allegations. Maybe so, but it is more likely to be a wind-up with Morrissey proving as oblique as ever. The sound of a revving motorbike (actually a chainsaw) ushers in an uneasy parallel between pop life and dangerous sport. In the final stanza, Morrissey switches to more personal territory, concluding the album with an allusion to obsessive love that would not have been out of place on an early Smiths album. The amplified drums of new boy Woodie Taylor brings this exceptional work to a dramatic close.

# WORLD OF MORRISSEY

ORIGINAL/CURRENT ISSUE: PARLOPHONE CDPCSD 163, FEBRUARY 1995

The second compilation of Morrissey's solo career proved a major disappointment for those who had hoped he might at last take the opportunity to feature those many rare singles only B-sides on an album release. Instead, the compilation was a rag bag of recent singles, fleshed out by tracks from 'Beethoven Was Deaf' and 'Vauxhall And I'. Previously, Morrissey and Smiths' compilations followed a clear logic, logging singles, B-sides and, in The Smiths' case, some rare radio sessions. With 'World Of Morrissey', however, all logic goes out the window in what seems a cynical and unimaginative record company marketing exercise. The only mystery is why Morrissey would allow his work to be issued in such a lazy and haphazard fashion.

What the casual purchaser gets is four tracks from the recently issued 'Vauxhall And I', three live cuts from 'Beethoven Was Deaf', the three tracks from the recently released single 'Boxers' and three further tracks previously available on single only. As if to sum up the wayward nature of this compilation they even include 'The Last Of The Famous International Playboys'. Maybe they'd forgotten that it was already available on the previous compilation, 'Bona Drag'. Prior to this, Morrissey's catalogue had been exemplary good value but this album betrays a catch-all mentality and mainstream marketing that does nobody any favours... least of all Morrissey.

One final thought. The title was obviously borrowed from the famous Decca compilations of years ago like 'The World Of... Billy Fury'. Generally, these were quick fire compilations put together without too much thought, care or attention. This work seems like a parody of those, but at least EMI had the decency to issue the album with a mid-price tag. The hope is that it will attract casual listeners and serve as a basement bargain introduction to Morrissey's work. In this respect alone, the album serves its function well. All the tracks included have been previously discussed, except the following:

## WHATEVER HAPPENS, I LOVE YOU

At least the album starts with the highlight of the entire set. Criminally placed as the extra track on the single 'Boxers', this gem was one of the most adventurous and musically interesting moments in recent Morrissey history. Eclipsing even much of 'Vauxhall And I', this track allowed the musicians full rein to use their imagination and the results are most impressive. Boz Boorer provides some expressive sax work, heightened by the use of sound effects and some strong rhythm work from Bridgwood and Taylor. The entire song has a distinct flavour of mid-period Yardbirds guitar work from Whyte, while Morrissey's vocal is both beguiling and passionate. One of the best ever Morrissey B-sides, this would have made a fine single in its own right.

## HAVE-A-GO MERCHANT

In common with its A-side 'Boxers', this revealed Morrissey's current penchant for singing about rough boys, complete with a line of pub cockney patter. Not the greatest Morrissey song, but a sound B-side and typical of the group sound he has developed on recent releases. The title displays Morrissey's affection for dated London slang, although some wily commentators maintain that it may be a coded slight directed towards Natalie Merchant who sang a cover of 'Everyday Is Like Sunday'.

## THE LOOP

Recently released in live form on 'Beethoven Was Deaf', this is the studio version which appeared on the 12-inch single and CD of 'Sing Your Life'. With all the rare single B-sides at their disposal, the compilers choose a track that is far less arresting than most of its rivals and which we've just heard live anyway. It merely makes you focus on all those that have been missed.

## BOXERS

The current single at the time of the compilation's release, this was Morrissey's paean to pugilists past with a snatch of commentary from, I think, Reg Gutteridge, among others. As boxing anthems go, this was far from one of the best and a less commercial single than we might have expected.

## MOONRIVER

This nine-and-a-half minute version of the Henry Mancini/Johnny Mercer classic had previously been a 1961 chart topper on HMV for Danny Williams. Familiar to anyone who has seen the film *Breakfast At Tiffany's*, the song has long been a standard and was a surprise choice by Morrissey who, for reasons of his own, changed the title from 'Moon River' to 'Moonriver'.

## MY LOVE LIFE

Something of a lost single from the Morrissey canon, this only reached number 29 despite the fact that it had never appeared on album. It was a reasonable, if unadventurous, single from the pen of Mark E. Nevin. Morrissey's lyrics are as slight as the arrangement, while the distinctive additional harmonies from Chrissie Hynde can be heard in the background.

Full track listing: *Whatever Happens, I Love You; Billy Budd; Jack The Ripper (Live); Have-A-Go Merchant; The Loop; Sister I'm A Poet (Live); You're The One For Me Fatty (Live); Boxers; Moonriver; My Love Life; Certain People I Know; The Last Of The Famous International Playboys; We'll Let You Know; Spring Heeled Jim.*

# morrissey
# cd singles

**M**orrissey's singles releases are rich in songs that have yet to appear on album. Despite the appearance of 'World Of Morrissey', a number of tracks are still locked away in the vaults and a substantial number can be found as extra tracks on CD. A glimpse at the below list reveals that these include 'Oh Well, I'll Never Learn', 'Sister I'm A Poet' (studio version), 'Michael's Bones', 'East West', 'Girl Least Likely To', 'At Amber', 'Tony The Pony', 'That's Entertainment', 'Skin Storm', 'Cosmic Dancer', 'I've Changed My Plea To Guilty', 'Pregnant For The Last Time', 'Pashernate Love', 'There Speaks A True Friend', 'Jack The Ripper' (studio version), 'You've Had Her', 'I'd Love To' and 'Interlude'. These alone would provide a rarities album, even without resorting to unreleased tracks or unissued live songs like the cover of Suede's 'My Insatiable One'. For the present then, a collection of Morrissey's CD singles is still requisite for those wishing to see the full picture.

Suedehead/I Know Very Well How I Got My Name/Hairdresser On Fire/Oh Well, I'll Never Learn
*HMV CD POP 1618 February 1988*

Everyday Is Like Sunday/Sister I'm A Poet/Disappointed/Will Never Marry
*HMV CD POP 1619 June 1988*

The Last Of The Famous International Playboys/Lucky Lisp/Michael's Bones
*HMV CD POP 1620 February 1989*

Interesting Drug/Such A Little Thing Makes Such A Big Difference/Sweet And Tender Hooligan (Live)
*HMV CD POP 1621 April 1989*

Ouija Board, Ouija Board/Yes, I Am Blind/
East West
*HMV CD POP 1622 November 1989*

November Spawned A Monster/He Knows
I'd Love To See Him/Girl Least Likely To
*HMV CD POP 1623 April 1990*

Piccadilly Palare/Get Off The Stage/At Amber
*HMV CD POP 1624 October 1990*

Our Frank/Journalists Who Lie/Tony The
Pony
*HMV CD POP 1625 February 1991*

Sing Your Life/That's Entertainment/The
Loop
*HMV CD POP 1626 March 1991*

Pregnant For The Last Time/Skin Storm/
Cosmic Dancer (Live)/ Disappointed (Live)
*HMV CD POP 1627 July 1991*

My Love Life/I've Changed My Plea To
Guilty/There's A Place In Hell For Me And My
Friends
*HMV CD POP 1628 October 1991*

We Hate It When Our Friends Become
Successful/Suedehead/I've Changed My
Plea To Guilty/Alsatian Cousin
*HMV CD POP 1629 April 1992*

You're The One For Me, Fatty/Pashernate
Love/There Speaks A True Friend
*HMV CD POP 1630 July 1992*

*Morrissey At KROQ.* There's A Place In Hell
For Me And My Friends/My Love Life/Sing
Your Life
*Sire 940184-2 October 1992*

Certain People I Know/Jack The Ripper/
You've Had Her
*HMV CD POP 1631 November 1992*

The More You Ignore Me The Closer I Get/
Used To Be A Sweet Boy/I'd Love To
*Parlophone CDR 6372 February 1994*

Hold On To Your Friends/Moonriver/
Moonriver (Extended Version)
*Parlophone CDR 6383 May 1994*

Interlude/(Extended)/(Instrumental)
*Parlophone CDR 6365 (**with Siouxsie**)July 1994*

Boxers/Have-A-Go Merchant/Whatever
Happens I Love You
*Parlophone CDR 6400 January 1995*

# johnny marr
## post-smiths albums

Following the break-up of The Smiths, Andy Rourke and Mike Joyce predominantly worked live, while seeking to form their own groups with a view to recording at a later date. Marr, meanwhile, became something of a session wizard, working with such artistes as Billy Bragg, Bryan Ferry, Talking Heads, Kirsty MacColl, Andrew Berry, The Pet Shop Boys, Stex And Banderas. He also toured with The Pretenders and played on their single, 'Windows Of The World'. His two major projects, however, were the CD albums he completed with The The and Electronic.

## the the
## MIND BOMB

ORIGINAL/CURRENT ISSUE EPIC 463319 1/2, MAY 1989.

Marr was originally invited to play guitar on the first single from this album, 'The Beat(en) Generation', but before the night was out, he decided to become a full time member of the group. As The The founder Matt Johnson explained to me: "It was almost the ideal band for Johnny and he always wanted to play with The The. I think it opened his eyes when he saw the way I worked. It does give you a lot of freedom whereas The Smiths, towards the end, was restrictive with the politics and everything else. That doesn't occur in my situation. If somebody bums me out, they're history. There's no problems or power struggles, which I can't bear. There may be some tension and electricity but, ultimately, that should be for bearing fruit. I'm not into mind games."

It should be noted that the majority of this album had been written before Marr's arrival and his compositional credit only stretched to one song, 'Gravitate To Me'. He did, however, receive a playing credit on the remaining tracks, excepting 'Armageddon Days Are Here (again)'. His playing throughout is far removed from his Smiths' work with a keener emphasis on expansive arrangements, minus those imaginative chord sequences of old. This proved Johnson's most bombastic and overwrought work and was a major disappointment after the brilliant 'Infected'.

There were some impressive moments though including the aforementioned single and 'Good Morning Beautiful' which Johnson claimed at the time was his best work. "I was really happy with what Johnny did on that," he enthused to me. "We were wielding the drugs at certain times to get the atmosphere, which is something I don't do so much any more. But some of the tracks we did that on, particularly 'Good Morning Beautiful', I filled Johnny up with drugs and said: 'This is Satan meets Jesus'. What he came up with was exactly what I wanted. It was superb. I was just filling up the multi-track with sound saying: 'Go again! Go again!' He could do all the things he wanted, without the usual confines of session work." Marr was

impressed and stuck around for a world tour and another album.

Full track listing: *Good Morning Beautiful; Armageddon Days Are Here (again); The Violence Of Truth; Kingdom Of Rain; The Beat(en) Generation; August & September; Gravitate To Me; Beyond Love.*

# DUSK

ORIGINAL/CURRENT ISSUE: EPIC EPC 472468, JANUARY 1993.

Despite his continued involvement with The The, Marr did not write any of the music on this album, which was entirely the work of Matt Johnson. However, Marr is credited for musical contributions to every track, bar 'True Happiness This Way Lies' and 'Bluer Than Midnight'. 'Dusk' proved a remarkable return to form, with Johnson coming to terms with a death in the family and producing some of the darkest and most uplifting music he has ever recorded. Marr compared the spirit of this album to John Lennon's primal scream exorcism with the Plastic Ono Band. Listening to it again, you hear what he means. The production by Johnson and Bruce Lampcov captures The

The at their most naked and arresting, with a clarity of sound that is exceptionally striking.

Full track listing: *True Happiness This Way Lies; Love Is Stronger Than Death; Dogs Of Lust; This Is The Night; Slow Emotion Replay; Helpline Operator; Sodium Light Baby; Lung Shadows; Bluer Than Midnight; Lonely Planet.*

# electronic

# ELECTRONIC

ORIGINAL ISSUE: FACTORY FACD 290, JUNE 1991.

Sandwiched between the two The The albums was Marr's major side project, the "mini-supergroup" Electronic. Originally, Marr had intended to guest on a solo album with New Order's Bernard Sumner but, in common with Matt Johnson, the project worked so well that they decided to make an album. With the assistance of The Pet Shop Boys, they recorded the Top 10 hit single, 'Getting Away With It'. Unfortunately, that track was not included on the original issue of the album, but was subsequently added to reissues. Work on this album dragged on for so long that some people believed it might never be completed. Four years after Marr's departure from The Smiths it finally appeared to critical acclaim.

The highlight was probably the single 'Get The Message', which included an evocative guitar opening, reminiscent of Marr's work with The Smiths. The remainder of the album was pretty solid, ranging from the accessible thrust of 'Tighten Up' and 'Idiot Country' to the expressive instrumental 'Soviet' and the engaging coda 'Feel Every Beat'. The involvement of The Pet Shop Boys on 'The Patience Of A Saint' added a pleasantly languid feel, despite the supergroup line-up. Marr insists that the Electronic experiment is far from over but it seems that the follow-up will take even longer to complete than its predecessor while a full scale tour would appear to be out of the question for the foreseeable future.

Full track listing: *Idiot Country; Reality; Tighten Up; The Patience Of A Saint; Gangster; Soviet; Get The Message; Try All You Want; Some Distant Memory; Feel Every Beat.*

# INDEX
## THE SMITHS

# MORRISSEY